seeing the SAVIOR in your scars

The Character of God in the Presence of Pain

By Grant Gaines

Copyright and Permissions

© 2020 by
Grant Gaines

All rights reserved. No part of this book may be reproduced in any form without permission in writing from the publishers, except in the case of brief quotations embodied in critical articles or reviews.

Unless otherwise indicated, Scripture quotations are from The Holy Bible, New International Version®, NIV® Copyright ©1973, 1978, 1984, 2011 by Biblica, Inc.® Used by permission. All rights reserved worldwide.

Scripture quotations marked (ESV) are from The Holy Bible, English Standard Version. ESV® Text Edition: 2016. Copyright © 2001 by Crossway Bibles, a publishing ministry of Good News Publishers.

Scripture quotations marked (NLT) are from The Holy Bible, New Living Translation, copyright © 1996, 2004, 2015 by Tyndale House Foundation. Used by permission of Tyndale House Publishers, Inc., Carol Stream, Illinois 60188. All rights reserved.

Editing: Stephen Fox
Cover Design: Bill Chlanda
Interior Design: Bill Chlanda

ISBN: 9798636022275
Imprint: Independently published

Contact information:
seeingthesavior@gmail.com

To my sweet Sars - I've had the time of my life with you.

"We love because He first loved us."
1 John 4:19

To the countless number of family and friends who
relentlessly showered us in prayer - Thank you!

"...The prayer of a righteous person is powerful and effective."
James 5:16

"...the church was earnestly praying to God for him."
Acts 12:5

CONTENTS

All Aboard 9

Lesson #1: 17
The depth of your scars is determined by the size of your God

Lesson #2: 25
The harder life hurts, the closer God gets

Lesson #3: 33
God's past determines your future

Lesson #4: 41
Pain has a purpose

Lesson #5: 53
Pain provides a platform

Lesson #6: 63
He's not penalizing you, He's preparing you

Lesson #7: 71
Perseverance is an attitude to adopt, not an action to take

Lesson #8: 83
Pain is the ugly wrapping paper on a beautiful gift

To be continued 95

Disturb us, Lord, when
We are too well pleased with ourselves,
When our dreams have come true
Because we have dreamed too little,
When we arrived safely
Because we sailed too close to the shore.

Disturb us, Lord, when
With the abundance of things we possess
We have lost our thirst
For the waters of life;
Having fallen in love with life,
We have ceased to dream of eternity
And in our efforts to build a new earth,
We have allowed our vision
Of the new Heaven to dim.

Disturb us, Lord, to dare more boldly,
To venture on wider seas
Where storms will show your mastery;
Where losing sight of land,
We shall find the stars.
We ask You to push back The horizons of our hopes;
And to push into the future
In strength, courage, hope, and love.

- Sir Francis Drake -1577

All aboard

"What comes into our minds when we think of God is the most important thing about us."
- AW Tozer

"Who is God?"

That's a question I had answered many times in my life. Being raised in a Christ-following, Bible-believing, Sunday school-attending home, I knew the "correct" answer to that question. I had sung my fair share of "In Christ Alone," highlighted my way through J.I. Packer's book *Knowing God*, and could even rattle off Exodus 34:6–7, "The Lord, the Lord, the compassionate and gracious God, slow to anger, abounding in love and faithfulness, maintaining love to thousands, and forgiving wickedness, rebellion and sin. Yet he does not leave the guilty unpunished" in response to that question.

But now this familiar inquiry carried far more weight than in the past. It was no longer a hypothetical question to answer in a sterile Sunday school setting but was quickly threatening to become an honest reality. "If everything falls apart in the next 15 minutes, who is God? Is He really in control? Is He really compassionate? Does He actually hear my prayers? Is He still going to be enough for me?"

These were the sobering questions I wrestled with at 11:10pm on March 18, 2019, as my 41-week pregnant wife, Sarah, was being rushed back to the operating room. Just 60 seconds earlier I was celebrating Sarah's water breaking and eagerly anticipating the arrival of our first daughter, Remi. But after a prolapsed umbilical cord threw "Plan A" completely out the window, a fury of nurses and doctors scrambled in to wheel Sarah out of our room to perform an emergency C-section. The final words I heard as the group sprinted away were now echoing in my head, "Stay here. We're going to try to save your daughter."

Those certainly weren't the words I expected to hear when I rolled out of bed that morning. I was prepared for, "Congratulations! She's beautiful!" not "We're going to try to save your daughter." But this was no time for mulling over shattered expectations, this was a time for prayer. And I don't mean "bedtime prayers" or "pre-meal prayers," I mean *prayer*. Like *desperate prayer*.

However, no matter how hard I gritted my teeth, clinched my hands, or squeezed my eyes, I couldn't shake the question, "Who is God? If the doctors aren't able to save Remi, or even Sarah for that matter, is Jesus still enough? Will God still be good? Will He still be in control?" This empty hospital room which was once so full of hope just one minute earlier had quickly been transformed into an interrogation room for my soul. *Who is God?*

You've been there before too, haven't you? Maybe it wasn't in hospital room #LRD2 but we've all had life throw us a curveball from time to time. You were expecting a wedding to plan but an unforeseen phone call left you with a heart to mend. You were expecting a routine doctor's visit to check off your list but a discouraging test result left you with a house to put in order. You were expecting a big bonus check to cash but were instead shown the door. You can be as prepared and even as "pre-prayed" as you want, but no amount of work or worship will save you from the gauntlet of life. Simply put pain affects us all—no one is immune. In the haunting words of John 16:33 (emphasis mine), "In this world you **will** have trouble."

It's in the hurt and heartache that we must each answer this all-encompassing question: *Who is God?* It's one thing to sing your answer in the church pews on Sunday, it's totally different ball game to be faced with this question when you're standing alone in a hospital room wondering what will become of your loved ones. If God doesn't save your spouse, your job, or your reputation, is He still on His throne? Is He still compassionate? Is He still close?

I wish I could tell you this book is all about my successful journey along the "pathway of pain" and three easy steps for you to do the same, but it's not. I wish I could tell you I never wavered from my Sunday school answer to the "Who is God?" question, but I frequently did. And I wish I could tell you I perfectly embodied James 1:2–3 during this trial ("Consider it pure joy...whenever you face trials of many kinds"), but that's sadly not the case either. I floundered A LOT during our time in the NICU (Neonatal Intensive Care Unit). I had doubts, fears, and went to bed more often than not with a lot of unanswered questions still racing through my head.

If you're looking for someone's footsteps to follow in, I'd recommend picking up a different book. Unlike the apostle Paul in 1 Corinthians 11:1, I can't confidently urge you to, "Follow my example, as I follow the example of Christ." My example leads to a cul-de-sac of doubts and disbelief. This book chronicles a faithless man struggling to follow a faithful God. I'm truly the last person who should write on this topic.

And yet, passages such as 1 Corinthians 1:26–31 among others seem to indicate this absolute unworthiness is exactly what the Lord is looking for. He likes to use our scars more than our successes. He uses our weaknesses to magnify His strength. He allows pain to be a far greater instructor than perfection. Therefore, in spite of all the assets I *don't* have, the one thing I *do* have seems to be exactly what the Lord is looking for – scars.

This particular season of scarring began when Remi was born at 11:21pm on March 18, 2019 with a tough uphill battle in front of her. A prolapsed umbilical cord led to an emergency C-section, two hospital transfers (including one by air), persistent pulmonary hypertension, pneumonia, necrotizing enterocolitis, renal artery stenosis, infantile polyarteritis nodosa, and finally, Takayasu's arteritis, all of which resulted in a six-week stay in the NICU. I honestly still don't fully understand what each of those conditions mean nor can I properly pronounce them. From what my wife tells me, Takayasu's arteritis is severe inflammation which threatens to completely block Remi's medium and large arteries.

While I'm no doctor, I do know what this disease leads to – scarring. Unfortunately, the physical scarring (and narrowing) of Remi's arteries is certainly an outcome of Takayasu's arteritis. But even more significantly, Takayasu's arteritis, as well as every other form of pain for that matter, all lead to spiritual, emotional, or relational scarring. Pain doesn't just come and go from our lives; it leaves its mark on our hearts. Every lost job, relationship, and physical disability leaves us as changed people with scars to show and stories to tell.

Therefore, this book is me rolling up my sleeves to show you my scars. Not because my scars in and of themselves are worthy of attention, but rather because of what, or should I say "Who" they point to. Every wound I received served as a teacher to instruct me, a professor to shape me, and a chaperone to lead me into a better understanding of who God truly is. No seminary class, book, or mentor has been as formative to my understanding of the Lord as those six weeks in the NICU were (and still continues to be). There is no question about it, we see the clearest picture of our Savior when we look back on our scars.

Even more significantly, every scar I received reminds me of the only scars worth focusing on – the scars of Jesus Christ.

Isaiah 53:5 says, "But [Jesus] was pierced for our transgressions, he was crushed for our iniquities; the punishment that brought us peace was on him, and by his wounds we are healed." My wounds may bring you momentary insight, but only Christ's wounds can bring you eternal salvation.

Consequently, this book is less of an autobiography of my story and far more of a celebration of His story. Specifically, the following pages highlight just eight (of the hundreds) of lessons I learned about the Lord and His character while sitting in the "school of suffering." You will certainly accompany our personal six-week journey through the NICU on the following pages, but the stories will be brief, timelines will be crunched, and details will be left out. I'm not trying to hide anything; I simply want to elevate Christ and make His character the center of this book.

Besides, the last thing you need when life hurts is a 300-page book to plow through. You don't need my words; you need His Word. I don't have an English degree to bolster my writing with, a seminary degree to rest my theological arguments on, or a wealth of life experience to draw from as I am still in my 20's as I pen this book (granted, upper 20's). My words can't even get my dog to submit; God's Word, on the other hand, cause creation, death, and Satan himself to fall in line. Knowing this, I want this book to be filled a whole lot more with the latter and far less with the former. So, if you're okay with it, I will do my best to be concise with my words while adding brushes of emotion and personal story only when they highlight the truths of God. Again, His story is the only one worth focusing on.

One way I attempt to achieve this brevity is by using each chapter title as a one-line summary of the rest of the chapter. If you want to save yourself time, flip to the table of contents, read each title, and put this book back on your shelf. As Albert Einstein once said, "If you can't explain something simply, you don't understand it well enough." I very deeply desire for this book to be simple, not sophisticated.

Finally, my goal in writing this book is not to compare spiritual scars. I may be young but I'm wise enough to know I'd lose that game. I in no way believe our trip down the "pathway of pain" has been any more difficult than yours. Our voyage certainly has been unique as doctors have told us Remi is by far and away the youngest known person with this disease in medical history, but I know there are a countless number of people who will read this book that would give ANYTHING to trade spots with me. I'm dealing with a sick child. Some of you have lost a child, a spouse, or so much more, that our journey looks like a plush Hawaiian vacation in comparison. You haven't just gone through the "school of suffering," you've earned your doctorate.

Please hear me loud and clear: this book is not me trying to compete with you, it's me trying to comfort you. Second Corinthians 1:3–4 (emphasis mine) tells us, "Praise be to the God and Father of our Lord Jesus Christ, the Father of compassion and the God of all comfort, who comforts us in all our troubles, **so that** we can comfort those in any trouble with the comfort we ourselves receive from God." In other words, the peace I received was intended to be passed along, not hoarded. Much like a gallon of Bluebell ice cream, God's comfort is at its best when it's shared with a group of loved ones.

This book is an attempt to do just that. I'm not writing because I'm an expert in this area, but simply a fellow sojourner with you along the "pathway of pain" who has tasted and seen the comfort of the Lord (Psalm 34:8). You could say this book is my "so that." Christ has allowed my family to go through this trying season **so that** His peace might flow through us to bless you. Who knows, perhaps the very reason Remi got Takayasu's arteritis in the first place was simply so that you can hold this book in your hand and be comforted by the truths of God's character.

My prayer is for the following pages to act like an aqueduct, transferring the infinite depths of God's peace from our hearts to yours. I'm praying for every wound we received during this season to be a powerful weapon of hope in your hand. I'm praying for my scars to equip you to answer the "Who is God?" question when you find yourself in your own valley. Most importantly, I'm praying for you to sense the presence of God more now than ever before. When life hurts, you don't need a book to read, you need a God to heal.

He's not just enough, He's more than enough.

"Yours, Lord, is the greatness and the power and the glory and the majesty and the splendor, for everything in heaven and earth is yours. Yours, Lord, is the kingdom; you are exalted as head over all."
- 1 Chronicles 29:11

Lesson #1:

The depth of your scars is determined by the size of your God

"The remarkable thing about God is that when you fear God, you fear nothing else, whereas if you do not fear God, you fear everything else."
- Oswald Chambers

Before Remi's birth, Sarah and I had discussed at great length our excitement for our first family photo. It's hard not to think about this moment when you live in today's social media-saturated world. You know the photo I'm talking about, don't you? It's a picture with a sweaty yet beautiful mom, a queasy yet proud dad, and a pink yet perfectly formed baby all huddled together moments after the baby's birth.

Unfortunately, with Remi's prolapsed cord and Sarah's emergency C-section, we never got the chance to take such a picture. Instead, after Remi was tended to for several hours following her birth and Sarah awoke from her medically-induced sleep, this was my precious wife's first look at the baby she so eagerly awaited to meet for 41-weeks:

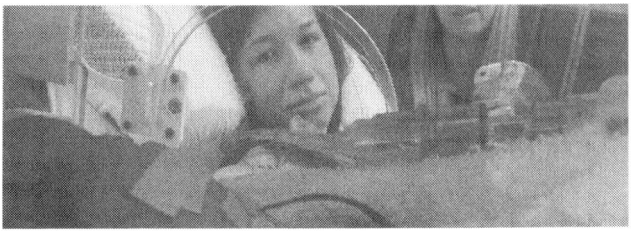

Heartbreaking, isn't it? Sarah was put under anesthesia with an unbridled anticipation for what this sweet child would look like and awoke to this. No smiles, cuddles, or kisses, just a sweet baby desperately hanging on for dear life. Everything Sarah and I had dreamed of was now surviving on life-support.

What do you do when you find yourself in this situation? When your hopes, dreams, and wishes are all hanging by a thread. What do you do when pain beats down the door of your life and makes itself at home in your heart? What do you do when life begins to leave scars?

The natural response is to size up our problems. "How big of a deal is this? How concerned should I be? How long will this take?" We size up our problems by asking these questions because we want to know what level of panic or peace we should proceed with. Big problems call for big concern; small problems require only a passing glance.

As logical and innocent as this approach may seem, most of our deepest emotional and spiritual scars are forged here. Choosing to measure your problems against the wrong standard such as numbers ("How much will this cost? How long will this take?" etc.) or experience ("Have I faced anything like this before? How common of an issue is this?" etc.) is to tie your heart to a "bucking bronco." The market will be up one day then down the next. A doctor will feel confident in the morning but unsure in the evening. And a politician will promise one policy today and enact a contradictory bill tomorrow. Nothing could be more volatile than numbers and experience.

I know this to be the case because this was the nauseating path I walked down during the first two weeks of this roller coaster (or "Remi coaster" as we affectionately call it) journey. Like a house of cards, my confidence was fragilely resting on the unstable foundation of probability ("What are Remi's odds?") and know-how ("Have the doctors seen this before?"). I can't even begin to describe the anxiousness I felt as we waited for the daily 9:00am doctor rounds to hear what Remi's "odds" were for that particular day. It was truly agonizing, believe me.

It wasn't until I was reading the Psalms one evening that I was able to get off this dizzying merry-go-round and size up my problems against the correct "Standard."

If you know anything about the book of Psalms, you'll recall it is a book from the heart for the heart. Unlike the apostle Paul's exhaustive, well-structured letters in the New Testament, the Psalms are messy, volatile, but most importantly, they're real. The authors aren't afraid to pull back the curtain to reveal what heartache truly looks like. You're not going to see a plastered smile, fake laughter, or insincere worship in this book; you're going to see an honest look at suffering, scars and doubts—lots of doubts.

This vulnerability caused the book's chief author, David, to become a dear companion to Sarah and me during this season. He knew what it was like to flirt with death, suffer loss, and patiently wait for the Lord. We felt as though we were reading the pages of our own journals as we flipped open to the Psalms and listened to the outpouring of David's heart. His pain was our pain and his prayers became our own.

I could relate with David's problems. I could relate with David's anxiety. What I couldn't relate with, however, was David's hope. I couldn't come to grips with how David and I could look at an equally daunting list of problems and draw completely different conclusions. What was I missing?

The following three Psalms answered my question:

> "Lord, how many are my foes! How many rise up against me; many are saying of me, 'God will not deliver him.' But you,

> Lord, are a shield around me, my glory, the One who lifts my head high." (Psalm 3:1–3)

> "Even though I walk through the valley of the shadow of death, I will fear no evil, for you are with me." (Psalm 23:4, ESV)

> "God is our refuge and strength, an ever-present help in trouble. Therefore we will not fear, though the earth give way and the mountains fall into the heart of the sea, though its waters roar and foam and the mountains quake with their surging." (Psalm 46:1–3)

David's problems loomed large when compared to odds or experience, but David had a far better "Standard" to measure his troubles against – the Lord. Foes beyond number may have surrounded him but they were no match for the Shield who protected him (Psalm 3). His circumstances may have been scary, but his Shepherd was good (Psalm 23). And the earth may have been crumbling, but his Shelter would not be shaken (Psalm 46). David wasn't concerned with *what* his circumstances looked like; he was only concerned with *who* his God was.

As long as David kept his eyes fixed on the grand nature of God, he could maintain hope no matter what the world threw at him because his God was BIG. How big? Big enough! Big enough to take down a nine-foot giant, big enough to unite a country, and big enough to forgive his sins. The size of David's God dwarfed his problems and empowered his hope.

Don't get me wrong, David's life was still hard and littered with scars. Giants were still tall, isolation still haunted the king, and foreign armies were still imposing. But when David measured his fears, losses, and loneliness against his God, his scars began to lose their sting. Even in the darkest of circumstances, David's high view of God muffled the pinch of pain. David wasn't bulletproof or calloused, he was simply confident his

God was bigger than his problems. The depth of his hope neutralized the depth of his heartache.

This realization led me to understand a foundational truth: the depth of my scars would be determined by the size of my God, not by the severity of my circumstances. That is to say, the sting of a given situation would be inversely related to how big I believed my God was. If I had a big God, I would have small problems. If I had a small God, I would have big problems. Takayasu's arteritis, radiation, and medical bills would only be scary if I incorrectly believed they were bigger than my God.

Howard Hendrix said it best: "The size of your God determines the size of everything." I couldn't agree more. Our perception of God determines *everything*. The arrows of the enemy are only concerning if you believe they are more powerful than the Shield that protects you (Psalm 3:3). The valley of the shadow of death is only scary if you believe your Shepherd is not able to safely navigate you to the other side (Psalm 23:4). And the storms of life are only frightening if you believe their fury is mightier than your Shelter (Psalm 46:1–3). Simply put: the size of your God determines the size of your problems.

Please notice what I'm saying. The size of your God determines the *size* of your problems, not the *presence* of them. Just because you believe God is big doesn't mean your issues will magically disappear. Look no further than Jesus Christ. No one had a bigger view *of* God and yet no one was given a bigger pain *from* God. Christ's perception of God didn't eliminate His scars, but it did alleviate His fears. In spite of the mind-boggling weight of bearing the sins of the entire world as He died on the cross in our place, Hebrews 12:2 says Jesus was able to endure the cross with "joy" because of the hope laid before Him. "Joy." Not "angst, agitation, or anxiety," but "joy." Talk about mind-boggling!

Christ's grand view of God and high hope of heaven changed everything for Him. He still had pain, but in the light of God's incomparable power, His scars lost their sting.

Though Sarah and I came nowhere close to embodying the same level of confidence as Christ and often focused more on our problems rather than our Provider, our puny mustard seed faith still managed to bring about a renewed outlook. Bad news was still "bad" news and heartache still hurt deeply, but in the moments when we focused on the all-surpassing greatness of God, we were able to see every new trial as yet another opportunity for the Lord to write a better testimony for our sweet little girl to share one day. Every earthly setback was just a divine setup for a better scar to show and a greater story to tell. It was as if every difficulty was just another invitation for us to look at the size of our God rather than the size of our problems.

I believe this is the mindset the Lord longs for all of His children to adopt. Rather than being so concerned with *what* our circumstances look like, we need to start being more concerned with *who* our Creator is. Yes, your situation may be dire. Yes, funds may be low. And yes, this is an extremely rare battle you're fighting. But do you know what? This isn't big, new, or scary for the Lord. He hasn't just seen this before; He foreknew it before the creation of the world. He's never been shocked or caught off guard. He's never been outmatched or outmuscled. No circumstance has ever caused God to shudder or wring His holy hands. He has always been and will always be totally in control of all things...including your scars.

Once we come to grips with this reality, all bets are off. Throw the measuring sticks of odds and experience out of the window. God doesn't play by probabilities; He plays by His own sovereignty. He doesn't submit to "We've never seen this before" or "There's nothing else we can do." He's able to do, "... immeasurably more than all we ask or imagine" (Ephesians

3:20). Though we've been blessed with common sense to navigate this life, we've been ultimately commanded to walk by faith, not by sight (2 Corinthians 5:7). We don't live by numbers but by, "...every word that comes from the mouth of the Lord" (Deuteronomy 8:3). The entire world may be against us, but God is actually for us—always (Romans 8:31)!

These verses bring encouragement only if you have a high view of God. Constantly throughout Scripture the Lord calms the fears of His children by promising His presence to be with them. He doesn't tell them not to fear because their circumstances aren't all that bad or the end of their trial is in sight, He simply assures them of His presence. Again, this is only comforting if you believe the God who is with you is bigger than the problems in front of you.

For example, if a fully-grown 420-pound lion was charging at me and the only thing standing between me and this man-eating "King of the Jungle" was my childhood chocolate lab, Maverick, I'm in trouble—BIG trouble. However, if this same lion was charging at me but standing between us is no longer a dog but a thick wall of bars and bullet-proof glass at the zoo, I would clap in excitement, not flee in fear. The level of my fear would be directly tied to the level of my confidence in the one who is defending me.

Or let's look at another example. I've always been told there are three kinds of people in the world: those who are good at math and those who aren't. I'm not sure which category I fall into, but I do know if you were to throw a math test in front of me right now, I would be rather uncomfortable and clueless. However, if I were to walk into this same math test with a partner by the name of Albert Einstein, I'm no longer going to be afraid. Why? Not because the questions are any easier or because I'm now well studied. I'm going to be confident simply because I believe the one who is with me is greater than the problems in front of me.

I could go on and on, but I think you get the point. Nothing could be more important than how big you believe your Defender is. The depth of your scars will be determined exclusively by this reality. Sickness, pain, loss, and even death may still be present, but in view of Christ's death-conquering resurrection, we stand firm and confidently say along with Paul, "Where, O death, is your victory? Where, O death, is your sting?" (1 Corinthians 15:55).

How big is your God?

> "Great is our Lord, and abundant in power;
> his understanding is beyond measure."
> - Psalm 147:5 (ESV)

Discussion Questions:

1. What fears are you currently wrestling with?
2. How might a proper view of God's grand character and infinite power neutralize these fears?
3. What are some Bible verses you can memorize in order to combat these lies?
4. How big is your God at this moment?

Lesson #2:

The harder life hurts, the closer God gets

*"I don't always feel His presence.
But God's promises do not depend upon my feelings;
they rest upon His integrity."*
- R.C. Sproul

Some realities in life logically rule each other out. For example, if you can read this sentence, you can't be illiterate. If you have a sibling, you can't be an only-child. And if you are a God-fearing, Spirit-filled Christian, you can't dislike dogs. The presence of one element rules out the other by its very nature. They simply cannot both be true at the same time.

Satan would love for you to believe that God and pain belong on this list. If pain is near, he whispers, God must be far. The two naturally rule each other out and consequently cannot be present at the same time. Therefore, if life is difficult, God must be distant.

This is a lie Satan loves to tell, and if I'm honest, he's really good at getting me to take the bait. It's hard to wrap my finite mind around the ways of an infinite God. *How could a loving and all-powerful God be near when pain is devouring my life?*

This lie may be easy to dissect when written on a piece of paper but it's rather difficult to deny when spiritual, emotional, and relational scars invade our lives. Satan even tricked David, you know, The-Man-After-God's-Own-Heart David, into this lie: "Why, Lord, do you stand far off? Why do you hide yourself in times of trouble?" (Psalm 10:1), "My God, my God, why have you forsaken me? Why are you so far from saving me, so far from my cries of anguish?" (Psalm 22:1), "Why, Lord, do you reject me and hide your face from me?" (Psalm 88:14).

Heartache has a way of blurring our senses and toying with our emotions. When life hurts it's hard to comprehend the nearness of God in the presence of pain. But this is where we must be careful. God never told us to base our understanding of Him on our emotions but on His Word. Satan may tell us that God's presence flees at the sight of pain, but what do the Scriptures say?

I desperately needed this question answered during the first three days of Remi's life. Hours after Remi was born, doctors determined she needed to be immediately transferred from our hospital in Branson to a hospital 45 minutes north for better treatment. To make matters worse, the transfer meant Sarah would be separated from Remi and me for three long days while she recovered in Branson from her traumatic emergency C-section.

While I wasn't totally alone in Springfield, those first three days were still unbelievably lonely. It was one thing to have my first child covered in more cords and tubes than I could count, it was all the more difficult to add a separated wife into that equation, too.

As is the case with every painful situation we go through, the scars I received during those first few days served as a breeding ground for Satan's usual slander – "*God doesn't care about you. He's not interested in your prayers. He's nowhere to be found!*" and so on. Satan used every setback and piece of bad news as more "proof" of the distance between me and my Savior. The harder life hurt, I was led to believe, the farther away God was.

This lie was particularly easy to fall for late in the evenings after my family left the hospital. I would stay by Remi's bedside until about 2 or 3am each morning looking at and praying over her. It was in those wee hours of the morning when the lies of Satan and the questions of my heart would shout most loudly, *"Where is God in all of this? Doesn't He see me? Doesn't He care?"*

Fortunately, however, as I was reading late one night the Lord used the truth of His Word to drive out the lies of the Enemy. I opened my Bible and came upon the familiar story of Shadrach, Meshach, and Abednego in Daniel 3. If you'll recall from your days in Sunday school, these three friends were thrown into a blazing furnace for refusing to bow to the idolatrous whims of King Nebuchadnezzar. While this was an unfortunate circumstance for the characters in the story, it was the perfect case study for me to examine. If these fears I was led to believe were actually true, then falling into a furnace would have been the equivalent of falling out of God's presence. Nebuchadnezzar's sentence would not only have seared these boys' clothes, it would have severed their proximity to the Lord.

But as I reread this familiar story through this new lens, I couldn't help but notice how their punishment didn't push them towards their death, it actually pushed them towards their God.

> "...and these three men [Shadrach, Meshach, and Abednego], firmly tied, fell into the blazing furnace. Then King Nebuchadnezzar leaped to his feet in amazement and asked his advisers, 'Weren't there three men that we tied up and threw into the fire?' They replied, 'Certainly, Your Majesty.' He said, 'Look! **I see four men** walking around in the fire, unbound and unharmed, and **the fourth looks like a son of the gods**'" (Daniel 3:23–25, emphasis mine).

The preincarnate Christ, whom many theologians believe was the fourth man Nebuchadnezzar saw in the furnace, did not turn a blind eye to these men when the flames rose all around them. He helped them. Even more than that, notice *how* He helped them.

The Lord could have very easily spoken a single word and the three friends would have been delivered, but He didn't do that. He could have sent a powerful rainstorm to extinguish the flames, but He didn't do that either. Instead, much like Garth Brooks, God was not satisfied merely "standing outside the fire." God wanted to be with the men *in* their suffering before delivering them *from* their suffering. God simply couldn't help Himself. The hotter the flames of destruction got, the closer the Father of Deliverance leaned in.

It would be easy to overlook this instance if this were the only example of God's presence in the midst of pain, but fortunately it's not. God has never been One to stand back and watch as His children suffer. Time and time again we see this reality play out: when hope seemed far, God drew near.

When the Lord liberated His children from 400 years of Egyptian slavery, He didn't just send His signs, He sent Himself – "I will be with you" (Exodus 3:12). When Samson was surrounded by 1,000 angry Philistines, God didn't just send His deliverance, He sent His Spirit – "[t]he Spirit of the Lord came powerfully upon [Samson]" (Judges 15:14). Most significantly, when the world was lost in the darkness of our sin, God didn't just send His law, He sent His Son – "For God so loved the world that gave his one and only Son, that whoever believes in him shall not perish but have eternal life" (John 3:16).

There aren't very many certainties in this life but one thing you can bank on is the nearness of the Savior in the midst of suffering. This principle is at the very heart of the Bible because it is at the very heart of the gospel. God didn't *pull* us out of sin,

He *carried* us out. He didn't save us from His heavenly throne, He saved us from His rugged cross. As pain encroached our lives, God indwelt our hearts.

This principle uniquely sets Christianity apart from every other religion because only in Christianity do you have a God who knows from personal experience what it's like to be tempted, to be rejected, and to be crucified. Hebrews 4:15 says of Jesus our great high priest, "For we do not have a high priest who is unable to empathize with our weaknesses, but we have one who has been tempted in every way, just as we are—yet he did not sin."

You've never experienced a temptation or pain where Jesus can't also say, "Yep, I've been there too." This enables Jesus alone, unlike any other religion's god, to sympathize with our sorrows and share in our scars. As John Stott accurately pointed out, "In the real world of pain, how could one worship a God who was immune to it?" Have you been poorly treated? He has too (Matthew 26:47—27:56). Have you lost a loved one? He has too (John 11:1–44). Have you been given a terminal diagnosis? He has too (Matthew 26:36–46). Because Jesus was, "...despised and rejected by men, a man of sorrows and acquainted with grief" (Isaiah 53:3, ESV), He is able to both connect with us and comfort us at a personal level.

As I sat in that dark and lonely hospital room late at night holding the hand of my ailing daughter, this refreshing truth was like a cold glass of water to my parched soul. Though Satan's lies still shouted loudly, God's Word continued to gently remind me of His truth. Pain doesn't drive the Lord away, it actually draws Him near. He's not just competent, He's close. He's not just a God of power, He's a God of proximity. He was not just a God who was on His heavenly throne, but a God who was by my side. He was big enough to command the cosmos but close enough to wipe my tears away. Truly, pain did far more to usher me into the presence of God than any Christian conference, Chris Tomlin worship album, or beautiful sunrise could ever dream of.

No wonder James 1:2 tells us to, "Consider it pure joy, my brothers and sisters, whenever you face trials of many kinds." Pain may chase away our comfort, but it can't chase away our God. He is close to us in the good times and even closer in the bad times.

Look back with me once more to Shadrach, Meshach, and Abednego's trip to the fiery furnace:

> "Then King Nebuchadnezzar leaped to his feet in amazement and asked his advisers, '**Weren't there three men that we tied up and threw into the fire?**' They replied, 'Certainly, Your Majesty.' He said, 'Look! **I see four men** walking around in the fire, unbound and unharmed, and the fourth looks like a son of the gods.' Nebuchadnezzar then approached the opening of the blazing furnace and shouted, 'Shadrach, Meshach and Abednego, servants of the Most High God, come out! Come here!' So **Shadrach, Meshach and Abednego came out of the fire**," (Daniel 3:24–26, emphasis mine).

Let me do a little math test with you. How many men were originally thrown into the fire? Three. How many did King Nebuchadnezzar see when he looked into the furnace? Four. How many did they pull out of the flames? Three. How many does that leave in the furnace? One.

I need you to know that no matter what "fiery furnace" you find yourself in during this lifetime, there is still One, the Lord Jesus Christ, who will be there with you. He wasn't lying when He promised, "Never will I leave you; never will I forsake you" (Hebrews 13:5, emphasis mine). "But what if I've sinned...yet again?" "*Never* will I leave you; *never* will I forsake you." "But what if all my family members and friends deserted me?" "*Nev-*

er will I leave you; *never* will I forsake you." "But what if...." "*Never* will I leave you; *never* will I forsake you."

Romans 8:35–39 sums up this truth the best:

> "Who shall separate us from the love of Christ? Shall trouble or hardship or persecution or famine or nakedness or danger or sword? As it is written:
>
>> 'For your sake we face death all day long;
>> we are considered as sheep to be slaughtered.'
>
> No, in all these things we are more than conquerors through [Christ] who loved us. For I am convinced that neither death nor life, neither angels nor demons, neither the present nor the future, nor any powers, neither height nor depth, nor anything else in all creation, will be able to separate us from the love of God that is in Christ Jesus our Lord."

It doesn't matter if you're sitting in the NICU or in a traffic jam, the Lord isn't just a big God ruling and reigning over us, He's "Immanuel" – God *with us* (Matthew 1:23). He leans in when our hearts hurt. Psalm 34:18 says, "The Lord is close to the brokenhearted and saves those who are crushed in spirit." If I could translate that verse into my own words, Psalm 34:18 would read: *the harder life hurts, the closer God gets*.

Satan may tell you the presence of pain means the absence of God, but if you look closely enough, you will find the Savior in the midst of your scars.

"Where can I go from your Spirit?
Where can I flee from your presence?
If I go up to the heavens, you are there; if I make my bed in the depths, you are there.
If I rise on the wings of the dawn,
if I settle on the far side of the sea, even there your hand will guide me, your right hand will hold me fast.
If I say, 'Surely the darkness will hide me and the light become night around me,' even the darkness will not be dark to you; the night will shine like the day, for darkness is as light to you."
- Psalm 139:7–12

Discussion Questions:

1. Why does God often feel so far away when life hurts?
2. What season of life led you to feel the closest to God?
3. How does knowing Jesus was tempted like you affect your own outlook in times of trial?

Lesson #3:

God's past determines your future

"In God's faithfulness lies eternal security." - Corrie ten Boom

As I write these words in the early fall of 2019, Tom Brady has been the starting quarterback for the New England Patriots for 17 seasons. Of those 17 seasons, he has led his team to the playoffs 16 times. Of those 16 playoff appearances, he has failed to advance to the second round of the playoffs only once. Under Brady's reign, the Patriots have made the AFC Championship game (the third round of the playoffs) 13 times, including an NFL record eight-straight years. Finally, with Brady as their starting quarterback, the Pats have advanced to nine Super Bowls and have won the championship game a whopping six times, making Brady the winningest quarterback in the history of football.[1]

In a similarly impressive fashion, Nick Saban has been the head football coach of the Alabama Crimson Tide for the past 12 seasons. Of those 12 years, Saban has won roughly 87% of the games he's coached and has failed to win 10 or more games in a given season only once (Saban went 7–6 in his first season at Alabama). To put that in perspective, in the 25 seasons prior to Saban's arrival, the Crimson Tide had a grand total of only nine seasons with 10 or more wins.[2]

---

[1] https://www.pro-football-reference.com/players/B/BradTo00.htm
[2] https://www.sports-reference.com/cfb/schools/alabama/coaches.html

Lastly, as we enter into the 2019–2020 NBA regular season, LeBron James has played professional basketball for 16 years. Of those 16 years, LeBron has been voted as an NBA All-Star 15 times (he failed to make the All-Star Game his rookie year), has made the playoffs 13 times, has won three NBA championships, and has accumulated an impressive 31 All-NBA awards, including four MVPs.[3]

Knowing all of these stats, if I were to ask if you think Tom Brady will lead the Patriots to the playoffs, if Nick Saban will win more than nine games, or if LeBron will get an All-Star bid next year, what would you say?

If you're smart (and unbiased), you would have no other choice but to look at the long history of production and assume that just as Brady has done in 94.1% of the seasons he's played in, Saban has done 91.6% of the seasons he's coached, and LeBron has done in 93.7% of the seasons he's suited up for, they will do it yet again in this upcoming season. Why would you bet against them? Surely Father Time will catch up with these guys sooner or later but just looking at the cold hard facts, you'd be insane not to pencil the Pats into the playoffs, Alabama into a 10+ win season, and LeBron into yet another All-Star appearance before the season starts.

The reason we have so much confidence in what these guys *will* do is because we look back at what they've already *done*. The best predictor of future behavior is past performance. Therefore, though there may not be a tangible promise to base our predictions on, there is an awful lot of data to inform our projections.

As silly as this analogy is, it was one I thought about frequently while we were in the NICU. I knew the Lord was a good,

---

[3] https://www.landofbasketball.com/nba_players/j/lebron_james.htm

sovereign, just, merciful, and gracious God, I just didn't know what this good, sovereign, just, merciful, and gracious God would do in Remi's situation. He had certainly done some impressive acts in the past, but what would He do in the future? More significantly, what would He do in *my* future? Would He exercise His power by healing Remi, or would He let her death be a scar to draw us closer to Him?

As much as I wanted to know the answer to this question, there was no Magic 8 Ball or horoscope to tell me how God was going to work this situation out. I certainly had the Bible to look at but the more I searched the Scriptures the more I was reminded of the death, sickness, and sadness that littered this Holy Book's pages. Just because people prayed fervently, tithed generously, and obeyed religiously there was still no guarantee life would work out for them on this side of eternity.

Jesus Christ Himself is the chief example of this reality. He never broke a command, missed an opportunity, or made a mistake throughout His lifetime and where did all this perfection take Him? To the cross! If even Christ's devotion couldn't deliver Him from heartache, what hope did we have?

As I was praying about (i.e., "complaining about") the uncertainties of Remi's future early on in the first week in the hospital, the Lord used the simple sports analogies above to re-orientate my outlook. I have no promises of Brady's future playoff success, but I do have common sense and a lot of stats to bolster my confidence. I can't look into a crystal ball to see how well Saban's team will perform this upcoming season, but I can look backwards at his track record to find some assurance. And I don't know how well LeBron will play next year but because he hasn't missed the All-Star game in 15 years, wisdom tells me to assume his streak will continue.

The absence of a promise may bring an element of uncertainty but when you have a long track record to look at, this uncertainty brings anticipation, not anxiety. Fans of Tom Brady, Nick Saban, and LeBron James have confidence late in the 4th quarter of a close game not because they know the future outcome but rather because they have a slew of past outcomes to rest their hope in. Again, the best predictor of future behavior is past performance. Because these guys have pulled through so often in the past, one can only assume they'll do so again in the future.

This concept seems to be what the prophet Hanani was trying to communicate about God to King Asa in 2 Chronicles 16. The kingdom of Judah had recently witnessed the Lord conquer, against insurmountable odds, a ferocious Cushite army just two chapters earlier (2 Chronicles 14:9–15) and were now facing yet another sizable opponent. Despite the Lord's recent history of deliverance, Asa was terrified at the quickly approaching enemy and sent for help from the King of Aram rather than the King of heaven.

Second Chronicles 16:7–9 (emphasis mine) picks up on the action:

> "At that time Hanani the seer came to Asa king of Judah and said to him: 'Because you relied on the king of Aram and not on the Lord your God, the army of the king of Aram has escaped from your hand. **Were not the Cushites and Libyans a mighty army with great numbers of chariots and horsemen? Yet when you relied on the Lord, he delivered them into your hand**. For the eyes of the Lord range throughout the earth to strengthen those whose hearts are fully committed to him. You have done a foolish thing, and from now on you will be at war.'"

Hanani was dumbfounded. How could Asa witness such a marvelous deliverance from the Cushites just two chapters earlier and now doubt God's ability to deliver him yet again? What in God's past lent any room for this doubt? Had He ever failed or let the king down? Had He ever been faithless or faltered in His promises? King Asa may not have had guarantee to latch onto, but he did have a track record t look back upon. The uncertainty of Asa's future should have been viewed through the filter of God's past.

This is exactly what David seemed to do right before famously taking down Goliath. Though he was young, small, and far less trained than his opponent, David had confidence to move forward because he first looked backward:

> "Saul replied [to David], 'You are not able to go out against this Philistine [Goliath] and fight him; you are only a young man, and he has been a warrior from his youth.'
>
> But David said to Saul, 'Your servant has been keeping his father's sheep. When a lion or a bear came and carried off a sheep from the flock, I went after it, struck it and rescued the sheep from its mouth. When it turned on me, I seized it by its hair, struck it and killed it. Your servant has killed both the lion and the bear; this uncircumcised Philistine will be like one of them, because he has defied the armies of the living God. **The Lord who rescued me from the paw of the lion and the paw of the bear will rescue me from the hand of this Philistine**'" (1 Samuel 17:33–37, emphasis mine).

While everyone else was mesmerized by the size of Goliath's stature, David was mesmerized by the size of God's track record. The Lord had rescued David from danger time and time again, why would this opponent be any different? What reason had God ever given him to doubt? Why wouldn't David assume the best? Because David saw his future showdown with Goliath through the filter of God's past, he had confidence to run, "...quickly toward the battle line to meet him" (1 Samuel 17:48).

This truth sunk right between my eyes much like David's stone sunk right between Goliath's. I may not have had a tangible promise to cling to, but I did have a tangible Bible to open. And while this Bible didn't give me a guarantee of Remi's future deliverance, it did give me over 2,000 years and 66 books of God's past track record. It didn't matter where I flipped to, every story shouted, "God is faithful!"

Just take a look at the Lord's stats – He hasn't been faithful for 17 years like Tom Brady, 12 years like Saban, or 16 years like LeBron, He's been faithful since before the sun began to shine. There has never been a situation in which He hasn't been in total control and done what was perfectly right. He has always provided what His children needed when they needed it. He is undefeated, unflustered, and undeterred in every aspect of existence. The cosmos still obey Him, the demons still submit to Him, and "the waves and wind still know His name."[4]

From Genesis to Revelation, every book, chapter, and verse of the Bible exists to declare the faithfulness of the Lord.

Though I didn't focus on this reality nearly enough while we spent our days in the NICU, I can't begin to describe the peace that flooded my heart when I did. Remi's future was (and still is) up in the air, but in light of God's past faithfulness, why on earth would I bet against the Lord showing up and showing off? Why would I sit here and assume my loving Father wouldn't heal the girl He knit together in Sarah's womb for nine months (Psalm 139:13–14) and sent His one and only Son to die for (John 3:16)? Given His stats and long history of faithfulness, wouldn't it just be irresponsible and illogical not to assume the best?

"Assuming the best" is simply a term I am using to describe the biblical concept of hope. Biblical hope, unlike worldly hope, is not a wishy-washy uncertainty of some future event – "I hope

---

[4] "It is well" - Bethel Music

the Cowboys win the Super Bowl. I hope we have Mexican food tonight. I hope she says 'Yes' when I ask her out." All of these are shots in the dark. Who knows how they will turn out?

Biblical hope, on the other hand, is the current assurance of a future event (see Hebrews 11:1). It is the 100% certainty of an outcome that is yet to take place. It is the confidence that the sun will rise tomorrow because it has never failed to do so since the dawn of time. In other words, the assurance brought about by biblical hope is not rooted in blind faith, but in God's immeasurably long track record. We have hope because we have a faithful God, not favorable circumstances.

Having hope leads us to view our frightful future through the lens of God's faithful past. When darkness seems to hide His face, we can rest in His unchanging grace.[5] When we can't trace His hand, we can trust His heart.[6] When uncertainties invade our lives, we can possess a hope-filled anticipation, not a heart-pounding anxiety. Simply put, having hope in God's past allows us to assume the best in the future.

This is in no way to say we can "assume our way" or "hope our way" into this better future. As we've discussed previously, there are countless numbers of examples of righteous people getting stuck with the short end of the stick in the Bible (i.e., Jesus). The last thing I want you to hear is that your cancer, broken marriage, or heartache can be "hoped" away if only you would adopt a certain level of faith. I'm asking you to assume the best because that's what God's track record demands, not because that's necessarily how healing occurs.

The reality is God might not help your marriage or heal your disease in the way you hoped. He might not "come through"

---

[5] "On Christ the Solid Rock" - Edward Mote
[6] "Trust His Heart" - Babbie Mason

on this side of eternity or affirmatively answer your prayers. The truth is our finite brains cannot fully grasp the infinite ways of the limitless God on this side of heaven (Isaiah 55:8–9). But until the chips fall where they may, and given all the times He *has* "come through" in the past, why should we guess this time would be any different? Why wouldn't we assume the best?

This is the hope Sarah and I desperately fight to cling to regarding Remi's health. An uncertain future continues to threaten our peace, but God's tried and true past solidifies our hope. He's eternally good and immeasurably powerful. He's always loving and always righteous. Therefore, though we have no promise of Remi's future restoration, we have confidence that, "Jesus Christ is the same yesterday and today and forever" (Hebrews 13:8). We may not know *what* He'll do, but we do know *who* He is. What a wonderful promise to trust in and bet our daughter's life on!

"I was young and now I am old, yet I have never seen the righteous forsaken or their children begging bread."
- Psalm 37:25

Discussion Questions:

1. Why is it so difficult to trust God with our futures?
2. Name one or two times you've personally seen God "come through" for you in the past?
3. What are some practical ways you can remind yourself of God's past faithfulness in times of trial (e.g., write out a list, create a worship playlist, etc.)?

Lesson #4:

Pain has a purpose

"The sovereignty of God is the pillow upon which the child of God rests his head at night, giving perfect peace." - Charles Spurgeon

For as long as pain has existed, the question "Why?" has plagued every heavy heart. "Why did they have to die so young? Why did I get this disease? Why did he treat me so poorly? Why, why, why?"

Job wrestled with this question in the Old Testament as he considered his sufferings, "**Why** have you [God] made me your target?" (Job 7:20, emphasis mine). The crucified Christ uttered this question in His dying hours, "My God, My God, **why** have you forsaken me?" (Matthew 27:46, emphasis mine). Even those who don't believe life has any purpose whatsoever long to find meaning for the hurt and heartache they experience. Wherever pain exists, the universal "Why?" question is sure to follow.

My "Why?" question laid largely dormant for the first two weeks in the NICU. I naively assumed Remi's stay at the hospital would be brief and we would be back at home living a normal life (or at least as "normal" of a life you can have once a baby enters the picture!) in a couple of days. I knew Remi had issues, but I assumed they were very manageable issues. Give her a little medicine and a little time, I supposed, and she'll be just fine! However, after Remi's heart rate and blood pressure refused to be tamed, the doctors in Springfield deemed it best for us to be transferred up to St. Louis Children's Hospital.

We were hardly in St. Louis for 24 hours before we were blindsided with the alarming news of Remi's most recent MRI scan. Sarah, myself, and both sets of grandparents sat in a crammed conference room while doctors explained the severity of Remi's condition. She didn't have a common cold or just a random series of unfortunate events, she had rapidly narrowing arteries which were threatening to shut down several of her vital organs. This was serious. This was a matter of life and death! If action wasn't taken immediately, sweet Remi might not make it through this.

Recognizing the weight of this news, the doctors kindly filed out of the room giving our family a chance to stay back and consider what we just heard. Reflecting on this diagnosis quickly turned into praying for deliverance which quickly turned into weeping uncontrollably. Unlike ever before this "Why?" question roared to the forefront of my mind. I simply couldn't suppress it any longer – *"Why does our little baby girl have to go through so much pain? Why us? Why now? Why, why, why?"*

At some point during this tear-muffled prayer session, I distinctly remember praying the mechanical response I had learned as a child in Sunday school when answering the "Why?" questions of life, "Lord, we don't need to ask 'Why?' because you've already told us why – *for our good and Your glory.*" After wrapping up our prayer, we hurried to Remi's bedside in an attempt to stop time and cherish whatever remaining moments we had with our daughter as our tears continued to flow.

Though the conference room was now behind us, the words I prayed in there still haunted me throughout the rest of the night: *"This trial is for my good and God's glory."* I knew this was the "correct" Christian answer to the "Why?" question, but now that "Why?" was no longer a theoretical Sunday school topic to discuss but a tangible reality to live through, I struggled mightily with this conclusion. It just didn't seem to satisfy. Sure, a statement like this would fit nicely on a coffee mug or on a bumper sticker, but at this moment? With this diagnosis? How on earth could the King of heaven use Remi's disease and our consequential pain for *my* good and *His* glory? I just didn't get it.

As I was wrestling with these questions, I decided I needed to go straight to the Source and check the validity of this statement in the first place. Did the Bible truly teach that every pain results in our good and God's glory or was this just a cute sentence I had memorized as a child? And if this concept was indeed true, what does this lofty idea look like when it's played out in real life? How did the characters in the Bible experience the glory of God and the good of mankind when their lives fell to pieces? Perhaps if I could first answer these questions, I reasoned, I might have a little more insight into how my own scars could result in my good and His glory.

Why did the Father harden Pharaoh's heart and not allow the Israelites to leave Egypt when they asked? Why did the Son allow Lazarus to die after his sisters asked Him to heal Lazarus while he was still alive? Why did the Spirit allow Stephen to be martyred though he did nothing but love God and serve others?

To help me answer these questions, I shifted my interrogation from, "Why DID God allow this to happen?" to, "What would we be missing if He DIDN'T allow this to happen?" In other words, what would we be missing if God protected the Israelites from Pharaoh's fury? What characteristic of Christ would we miss if He had healed Lazarus before he died? And finally, what would we be missing if the Holy Spirit diverted all the pain away from Stephen's life?

These hypothetical questions cultivated a childlike curiosity and unlocked a wealth of insight as I reexamined these familiar stories through a new set of eyes. These characters that I had always viewed as so stoic and untouchable took on a new form of mortality as I imagined them struggling with many of the same tough questions I was currently wrestling through. Let me begin with the Israelites' exodus from Egypt to show you what I discovered.

What would we be missing if the Lord had commanded Pharaoh to let the Israelites go without a fight? Why did He allow them to struggle for so long? God clearly states His purpose for their pain in Exodus 14:4 (NLT, emphasis mine), "And once again I will harden Pharaoh's heart, and he will chase after you [the Israelites]. **I have planned this in order to display my glory** through Pharaoh and his whole army. After this **the Egyptians will know that I am the Lord!**"

The Lord intentionally allowed His people to endure more punishment, more plagues, and more persecution because this was the route through which His name and His renown could receive the most glory. In other words, the Israelites' heartache was the avenue through which evangelism occurred. Their scars led to the Egyptians (and the whole world for that matter) seeing the Savior unlike never before.

Had the Lord allowed the Israelites to stroll out of Egypt without any struggle, the current generation of Israelites may have been amazed at God's power but that would have been it. The tales of this plague-less, semi-miraculous deliverance would have died with those men and women. Instead, the Lord stacked the odds so far against Himself that the nations couldn't help but pay attention when this ragtag bunch of slaves toppled the most powerful nation in the world without raising so much as a finger.

It was because of the Israelites' suffering and God's ensuing deliverance that the inhabitants of Jericho still trembled some 40 years after the exodus upon hearing the Lord's people were at their doorstep (Joshua 2:9–12). It was because of this same event that 1 Samuel 4:8 records the Philistine army screaming, "We're doomed! Who will deliver us from the hand of these mighty gods? They are the gods who struck the Egyptians with all kinds of plagues in the wilderness," roughly 500 years after the Red Sea was parted. It was because of the dramatic exodus that Nehemiah, one of the last major characters in the Old Testament, was able to pray: "You saw the suffering of our ancestors in Egypt; you heard their cry at the Red Sea. You sent signs and wonders against Pharaoh.... **You made a name for yourself, which remains to this day**," 1,000+ years after the Israelites' departure (Nehemiah 9:9–10, emphasis mine). And it is because of this remarkable event that millions of Jews make it their annual habit of celebrating the Passover still to this day (roughly 3,000 years post-exodus).

God's purpose in the Israelite's suffering was to bring about the most glory for Himself and the greatest good for mankind. Mission accomplished? I think so!

On a more personal level, had this story never been recorded in the Bible I would have no idea just how powerful my God truly is. For just as the strength of an Olympic power lifter is measured by the amount of weight they can bear, so the power of God is measured by the amount of resistance He can overcome. Had Pharaoh let the Israelites walk without a fight, what strength would that have proven? More significantly, who could relate with such a fairy-tale story where everything went perfectly as planned? In the heat of our own trial, when nothing seemed to be going our way, I so desperately needed to know that even the most powerful scheme of man was no match for the almighty King of heaven and earth. "I know that you can do all things; no purpose of yours can be thwarted" (Job 42:2).

And what about Lazarus? What if Jesus healed him the moment Lazarus's temperature rose above 100 degrees? What would we be missing? John 11:5–6 gives us our answer:

> "Now Jesus loved Martha and her sister and Lazarus. So when he heard that Lazarus was sick, he stayed where he was two more days."

Surely there was a typo, wasn't there? It should read, "Jesus loved Martha and her sister and Lazarus. **BUT**, when he heard Lazarus was ill, he stayed where he was two more days." Or even better, "Jesus loved Martha and her sister and Lazarus. So when he heard Lazarus was ill, he went to him **immediately**."

But the text doesn't read this way, does it? Instead, John 11:5–6 (emphasis mine) says, "Now Jesus loved Martha and her sister and Lazarus. **So** when he heard that Lazarus was sick, he stayed where he was two more days."

Wait, let me get this straight. Jesus's love for Mary and Martha caused Him to purposefully ignore their cries for help? That doesn't make any sense. Why did Christ do this?

It doesn't make sense if we only focus on Lazarus's comfort. However, as we'll soon see, Jesus wasn't as concerned with Lazarus's momentary comfort as He was for the community's eternal salvation. He didn't want people to think He was merely a good doctor who could heal the sick but "...the resurrection and the life" (John 11:25) who has power over death and the grave. To do this, He didn't need a sore throat to heal but a dead body to raise. Therefore, in love, He waited.

What became of this divine delay? I'm glad you asked. John 11:45 tells us that Lazarus's death and resurrection led to, "...many of the Jews who had come to visit Mary, and had seen what Jesus did, believed in him." Lazarus's physical death resulted in spiritual life for many. Had Jesus healed Lazarus before he died, none of this would have happened. For the second time in my brief survey of biblical trials, I witnessed yet another season of suffering resulting in the glory of God and the salvation of souls.

LESSON FOUR

How precious this truth was to me as Remi flirted with death time and time again. I was comforted by the reminder that even death and the grave are subject to my Savior's will. The Grim Reaper can't come near my daughter without my God's permission. "Where, O death, is your victory? Where, O death, is your sting?" (1 Corinthians 15:55).

And finally, we get to Stephen. Though Stephen may not get as much "airtime" as guys like Peter, Paul, and James on the pages of the New Testament, what we do know about him is quite impressive. According to Acts 6:3, 5, 8 (ESV), Stephen was a man, "...of good repute, full of the Spirit and of wisdom...a man full of faith and of the Holy Spirit" and was, "...full of grace and power, [as he] was doing great wonders and signs among the people." Not a bad résumé, huh?

Yet, despite his commendable character and stellar speaking skills (see Acts 7:1–53), Acts 7 ends with this tragic narrative:

> "Now when [the religious leaders Stephen had just condemned for killing Jesus] heard these things they were enraged, and they ground their teeth at him.... Then they cast him out of the city and stoned him.... And falling to his knees he [Stephen] cried out with a loud voice, 'Lord, do not hold this sin against them.' And when he had said this, he fell asleep [that is, he died]" (Acts 7:54, 58, 60, ESV).

Talk about an abrupt ending to a promising life! All Stephen did was love God and serve others, why such a harsh death? More importantly, what would we be missing if the Lord spared this saint of his enemies' stones?

One only needs to read the opening verses of the following chapter to find an answer to these questions:

> "On [the day Stephen was killed] a great persecution broke out against the church in Jerusalem, and all except the apostles

were scattered throughout Judea and Samaria.... Those who had been scattered preached the word wherever they went" (Acts 8:1, 4).

Stephen's death gave life to Christ's commandment from Acts 1:8: "But you will receive power when the Holy Spirit comes on you; and you will be my witnesses in Jerusalem, and in all Judea and Samaria, and to the ends of the earth." Prior to the stoning of Stephen, the gospel message remained largely planted in one place — Jerusalem. The disciples were comfortable, were at home, and apparently had no intention of getting this worldwide mission started anytime soon.

That is, of course, until persecution entered the scene.

No longer was it "safe" or remotely comfortable to be a Christian in Jerusalem because a man named Saul, "...began to destroy the church..." and was, "...breathing out murderous threats against the Lord's disciples" (Acts 8:3; 9:1). Rather than going the way of Stephen, Christ's followers fled the city and inevitably took the gospel message with them wherever they went.

Had the Lord spared Stephen's life and shielded the church from persecution, the early Christians would have likely lingered in Jerusalem rather than making disciples of all nations as they had been commanded (Matthew 28:18–20). In other words, the reason there are people in the 21st century from all over the world worshipping a Messiah from the tiny nation of Israel is in large part because of Stephen's fatal scars. His wounds essentially launched the early church and sent the gospel our way. Possibly to an even larger degree than the other two examples we've looked at, Stephen's suffering resulted in the greater good and the glory of God.

But this is where Stephen's story diverts from the other two. The Israelites had the luxury of seeing God's purpose for their pain after the Red Sea enveloped the Egyptians. Lazarus had the blessing of witnessing many of his neighbors put their trust in Christ as a result of his "dance with death." But Stephen, on the other hand, had no such privilege. While countless numbers of people were coming to salvation and churches were sprouting up all over the Mediterranean coastline, Stephen's family and friends were left with a disfigured body to bury and a broken heart to bear. They never got to see the "Happily Ever After" ending to this trial like the Israelites and Lazarus did; they simply saw the brutal murder of their beloved and likely assumed this was where his story ended.

Isn't this how life sadly plays out more often than not? Very rarely do we get to see a linear "A+B=C" answer to our "Why?" questions like the Israelites or Lazarus did. Instead, much like Stephen's family, when the dust settles, all we're left with is more questions to answer and more tears to tend to. The medicine didn't work, the bills didn't get paid, or the friend never showed up. It's in these "Stephen-like" moments of darkness when we must rely on the light of God's character and trust His unblemished track record of faithfulness (see Lesson #3). After all, as Acts 7—8 makes abundantly clear, just because we never see God's purpose for our pain doesn't mean He doesn't have a purpose. He always has and always will use every situation to bring about His ultimate glory and the greatest good.

This realization allowed Sarah and I to have hope knowing even Remi's pain would serve a greater purpose than we could ever see or imagine. For just, "As the rain and the snow come down from heaven, and do not return to it without watering the earth and making it bud and flourish...so is my [God's] word that goes out from my mouth: It will not return to me empty, but **will accomplish what I desire and achieve the purpose for which I sent it**" (Isaiah 55:10–11, emphasis mine). God's purpose and plans, much like the rains that water the earth, *never* return void. Whether or not we see their fruit on this side of eternity, they always, always, always result in the glory of God and good of mankind.

Because we have this assurance, James 1:2–3 (emphasis mine) tells us we can, "Consider it pure joy, my brothers and sisters, whenever you face trials of many kinds, because **you know that the testing of your faith produces perseverance**." Similarly, 2 Corinthians 4:16–17 (emphasis mine) says, "Therefore we do not lose heart. Though outwardly we are wasting away, yet inwardly we are being renewed day by day. For our light and momentary **troubles are achieving for us an eternal glory that far outweighs them all**." We have joy not because trials in and of themselves are grand but rather because we know our trials are actively accomplishing something. In other words, our joy in trials springs from our understanding that pain has a purpose.

This is not an idea unique to Christianity, it's actually common sense. Let me illustrate. If someone randomly asked you to chop off your arm for no good reason, would you? Certainly not! But now if your lifelong trusted doctor came to you and said they need to surgically remove your arm to keep a deadly cancer from spreading to the rest of your body, would your outlook on this amputation change? Absolutely! The procedure would be the same and the pain would still be present, but knowing it served a greater purpose would bring great solace to your suffering. The doctor was only hurting you momentarily so you might be healthier in the long run.

I believe this is how the Lord longs for us to view pain. It's not fun or pleasant but it does in fact have a purpose: the glory of God and the good of mankind.

What this ultimately means, then, is that pain is more of an *invitation* rather than an *obstruction* to God's greater story. The "Takayasu-moments" of life are meant to propel us forward, not knock us back. Though we don't get to see the pieces of the puzzle come together nearly as often as we would like, the story of Stephen among many others in the Bible remind us that, "...in **all things** God works for the good of those who love him, who have been called according to his purpose" (Romans 8:28, emphasis mine). There's not a purposeless pain or a single scar that exists outside of this God-ordained promise. ALL things – including the Holocaust, natural disasters, 9/11, your cancer, your loneliness, and the like – ultimately result in the glory of God and the good of His people.

This understanding alone moves our line of questioning from an accusatory, "Why?" to an earnest, "What?" – "<u>What</u> do You have in store for me, God? <u>What</u> are You trying to teach me? <u>What</u> good are You going to bring about because of this pain?" In other words, grasping the infinite nature of God's sovereignty – even over our deepest scars – is what ultimately brings hope to hopeless situations. He has all the power and He has a perfect purpose for your pain. What a blessed assurance to rest in!

> "You intended to harm me, but God intended it for good
> to accomplish what is now being done, the saving of many lives."
> - Genesis 50:20

Discussion Questions:

1. Why is it so hard to believe that every pain has a purpose?
2. What's one example from your own life where God turned a painful situation into a God-glorifying situation?
3. Are there any scars you bear whose purpose you're still waiting to discover?

Lesson #5:

Pain provides a platform

"It is doubtful whether God could ever bless a man greatly until He has hurt him deeply." – A.W. Tozer

Two weeks after Remi's first CT scan in St. Louis, it was time for another round of imaging. *This* would be the time we would see God's miraculous healing in Remi's sweet little body, I was sure of it. We went to bed the night before giddily talking about the potential of bringing our precious girl home for the first time in the near future. Four weeks was long enough in the NICU. We were ready to finally sleep in the same room as our baby and get away from all the chimes and beeps of her hospital room. Like Dorothy famously said, "There's no place like home!"

But these dreams didn't last long. Another MRI led to another conference room meeting with more doctors who found more narrowing in Remi's arteries. There was no chance of us going home any time soon. More significantly, our little girl's health wasn't improving like we had prayed. We came into the conference room with high hopes, we left with low expectations. The little girl we had fallen in love with over the past four weeks was slowly fading.

The 50-yard walk back to Remi's room was filled with heavy silence and blank stares. It felt as though we were literally watching Remi's precious life quickly slip through our fingertips and there was nothing we could do about it. We were absolutely dejected and totally desperate. There was no semblance of strength or joy radiating from our faces; we were beaten, bruised, and broken.

Upon our arrival back in our sweet daughter's room, Remi's nurse offered her condolences for the disheartening MRI results. I shrugged off the comments but Sarah, through her tears, explained that though our hearts hurt deeply we still had hope because of the God we followed. Life was hard but God was good.

Though their conversation was short and was often interrupted with tears, I couldn't help but notice how intently Remi's nurse listened to my wife's words. Her focus wasn't due to Sarah's joy, for her beautiful smile had been replaced with broken sobs. It wasn't because of Sarah's confidence, for that had crumbled back in the conference room. And it certainly wasn't because of Sarah's robust dissertation, for her words were frail and few. The only reason Sarah's message seemed to now resonate more than ever before was because of her brokenness, not in spite of it. It's as if Sarah's tears magnified her message.

After their conversation wrapped up, we left the hospital for yet another crushing car ride "home" without our precious little princess in the backseat. We ate dinner, spent some time praying through the Psalms, then, as was her custom, Sarah posted an update on social media. Her post was nothing fancy – just a simple summary of the MRI we received several hours earlier as well as a brief update on our own hearts. Life was hard but God was good.

Because I'm not on social media, I'm typically in the dark as to what my wife posts, but not this evening. A mere few seconds after Sarah published her update, my phone began to light up with concerned friends and valiant prayer warriors. Based on the volume of texts and content of their words, I assumed Sarah had posted a five-point sermon on suffering,

LESSON FIVE

overtly explained the gospel, or perhaps had given an altar call, but she didn't. She was simply honest about our hurt while being forthright about our hope. Our situation was not good, but our God was.

As I read text message after text message of people being moved, encouraged, and touched by Sarah's heartbroken yet hope-filled words, I couldn't help but recall the conversation with Remi's nurse earlier in the day. In both instances, our hearts were at their lowest, but our influence was at its highest. This influence didn't spring from well-structured sentences, winsome words, or a parade of passion, but from heartbreak, pain, and distress. It seemed as though now, in the most scar-filled moment of our lives, the words we spoke had the largest platform to stand on.

Pain universally has this effect. Whether it is the loss of health, loss of a job, or loss of a loved one, mankind has been wired by God to have compassion for the hurting and sorrow for the scarred. For example, what do you do when you see a car wreck on the side of the highway? You don't glance down at the radio to change the music – you slow down to look at the damage. What do you do when there's a massive hit in a football game? You don't take a bathroom break – you watch slow motion replays. And what do you do when you see Rocky thrown around like a ragdoll by Drago in *Rocky IV*? You don't yawn in boredom – you lean forward in anticipation. Why do we do all of these things? Because pain is to mankind what bright lights are to bugs – we simply can't help but be drawn in.

Perhaps this is one of the reasons the Lord allows pain into our lives. In His infinite wisdom He knows pain is hard for the onlooking world to turn away from, making it the perfect package to deliver the good news of Jesus Christ in. Far more than knowing how to become famous, skinny, or rich, people want to know how to endure pain. Your broken leg or broken

55

marriage is simply the intersection in which the curiosity of man and the good news of God can meet. After all, pain doesn't discriminate; it affects people from every tribe, tongue, and nation. Therefore, pain, much like the Trojan horse, is able to deliver gospel hope to people and places in a way no Billy Graham crusade could ever imagine.

If you don't believe me, lend your ear to the prophet Daniel and this Jewish boy from the nation of Israel will tell you that even in the foreign land of Babylonia where words don't translate, pain does.

The primary example of this reality takes place just three short chapters after Daniel's friends — Shadrach, Meshach, and Abednego — were thrown into the blazing furnace for their devotion to the Lord. Following a similar storyline, Daniel 6 recounts the time when Daniel, much like his friends, was exposed to the fiery wrath of a king for obeying the commandments of his God. Namely, Daniel refused to cease praying though he knew the punishment for his continued piety would be death by lions. His persistent prayer left King Darius with no other choice but to seal Daniel's fate by sealing him inside the lions' den.

But the powerful lions were no match for the all-powerful Lion of Judah. The kings of the jungle humbly submitted themselves to the King of kings by refusing to lay a paw on the Lord's anointed. The next morning Darius rushed to what he assumed was Daniel's eternal resting place only to discover his long-time advisor sleepily rubbing his eyes after a comfortable night of rest.

Although Daniel had been a faithful servant for nearly 70 years up to this point, only now did his faith have a platform to stand on and a captive audience to preach to. It wasn't a powerful position that opened King Darius's eyes to the message Daniel had been living out for almost a century, it was a trip to the

LESSON FIVE

lions' den. Successes and shrewd political moves did nothing more than cause Daniel's message to go in one ear and out the other. His scars, on the other hand, left their mark on King Darius's heart as can be seen from his subsequent decree:

> "Then King Darius wrote to all the nations and peoples of every language in all the earth: 'May you prosper greatly! I issue a decree that in every part of my kingdom people must fear and reverence the God of Daniel. For he is the living God and he endures forever; his kingdom will not be destroyed, his dominion will never end. He rescues and he saves; he performs signs and wonders in the heavens and on the earth. He has rescued Daniel from the power of the lions'" (Daniel 6:25–27).

I'm not sure if King Darius will be in heaven, but if he is, it will be because Daniel's trip to the lions' den rescued this pagan king from a trip to Satan's. One man's pain led to another man's salvation.

If you fast-forward a couple hundred years you will stumble upon more pain-produced gospel progress in the New Testament. Though the apostle Paul was not in a lions' den like Daniel, he was nonetheless locked up in a dark and damp Roman dungeon during the prime of his ministry. The apostle who once planted churches and ministered to the masses was now restricted to a tiny cell and a handful of guards. However, despite all of these limitations, restrictions, and inconveniences (i.e., "pains"), Paul joyfully wrote the following in Philippians 1:12–14 (emphasis mine):

> "Now I want you to know, brothers and sisters, that what has happened to me [Paul's imprisonment] **has actually served to advance the gospel**. As a result, it has become clear throughout the whole palace guard and to everyone else that I am in chains for Christ. And because of my chains, most of the brothers and sisters have become confident in the Lord and dare all the more to proclaim the gospel without fear."

Though Paul was in chains, his message was not (2 Timothy 2:9). What the Roman officials assumed would silence the apostle only served as a platform to advance his gospel. Paul not only preached constantly to the palace guards who were assigned to watch over him, his unwavering hope created a contagious boldness for onlooking Christians to emulate. In a large way, pain was the midwife of Paul's ministry. It was his imprisonments and thorns (2 Corinthians 12:9) that led to so much progress. These alignments may have robbed him of his freedom, but they didn't rob him of his influence. They only magnified it.

We can keep flipping all over the Bible and see more examples of this reality. The enslavement of Joseph in Genesis 37 didn't end his life, it saved his family's. The persecution of the early church in Acts 8 didn't squash its message, it spread it. Most significantly, the cross of Christ didn't end His ministry, it fulfilled it.

If these stories teach us anything, it's that pain provides a platform for the gospel to be preached and hope to be spread. C.S. Lewis put it this way, "Pain insists upon being attended to. God whispers to us in our pleasures, speaks in our consciences, but shouts in our pains. It is His megaphone to rouse a deaf world." Our deepest hurts preach the loudest sermons. Success may drown God's voice out, but pain amplifies it.

While this is certainly true, the reason we often fail to take advantage of this opportunity is because of one simple and self-evident reality: pain hurts.

Now I know I'm not breaking any news when I say pain hurts, but the monotonous nature of life tends to lull us to sleep to this reality. Rather than living with a "wartime" mentality like the Bible urges us to possess, we cozily live as though we were at peace all the while forgetting, "Your enemy the devil prowls around like a roaring lion looking for someone to devour" (1

Peter 5:8). Consequently, when scars invade our lives, we're caught off guard.

We can sit here and talk about how we want to leverage our pain like Paul and Daniel all we want but as the great "theologian" Mike Tyson once famously said, "Everyone has a plan until they get punched in the mouth." No wonder 1 Peter 4:12 pleads with its audience, "...do not be surprised at the fiery ordeal that has come on you to test you, as though something strange were happening to you." No wonder Jesus urged His disciples five separate times in one short chapter to "be on guard" and "stay awake" (Mark 13:9, 23, 33, 35, 37, ESV) when warning them of the catastrophic pain that was quickly approaching and the ensuing platforms this pain would soon provide.

Unless we heed these warnings and acknowledge that life WILL be difficult, pain will punch us in the mouth and knock us off our feet. Like the unsuspecting soldiers at Pearl Harbor, assuming this world is a plush Hawaiian vacation will lead to a rude interruption when pain inevitably invades our lives. Our best intentions will go out the window as self-preservation will overtake gospel-manifestation. Rather than fixing our eyes outward on the people we could be sharing with or upward on the mission the Lord might have for us, we will fix our eyes inward at all the hurt and pain we are experiencing.

I know this to be the case because in spite of all the overt John-16:33-type examples I read in the Bible — "In this world you **will** have trouble" (John 16:33, emphasis mine) — March 18th (the day Remi entered the world) and the pain that followed caught me off guard causing me to make Remi's hardship more about my hurt than my hope. Takayasu's arteritis provided a God-given, pain-produced platform and a blisteringly loud "megaphone" but it was far easier to use this platform to look inward than to look upward or outward. It was far more natural to use this "megaphone" to talk about the broken state of my heart rather than the beautiful Source of my hope.

But can I tell you what I learned from that season of self-centered suffering? The longer we stand in the spotlight, the less impact we will make. We may receive some momentary sympathy, but we will fail to have eternal significance. More people may begin to follow our story, but less people will fall in love with Christ's.

The bottom line is you won't see the gospel advance like the apostle Paul if you use your platform to herald your hurts rather than proclaim your peace. You won't see lifelong family members, friends, and colleagues suddenly "get it" like King Darius did if you use your scars to tell people about your suffering rather than your Savior.

This doesn't mean you need to grit your teeth and whistle "Zip-a-Dee-Doo-Dah" like nothing is wrong. No one can relate to that. After all, it's our pain that people empathize with, not our perfection, remember? Instead, what I'm suggesting is we share our hurt but never leave out the Source of our hope. Yes, this is a difficult diagnosis. Yes, the bills are stacked high. And yes, relationships can be rough. But do you know what? You can still proclaim a "living hope" because you still have a "Living Savior" (1 Peter 1:3). Life may be hard, but God is still good.

This is especially true when our prayers don't "survive the lions' den" like Daniel did. It's certainly noble and proper to proclaim hope after a resurrected marriage or resolved illness, but do you know what's even more impressive and attention-grabbing? When God doesn't heal your marriage, take away your cancer, or soften your scar and yet you still hold onto a death-conquering hope.

This hope-filled, God-centered suffering will make your message stand out like a lighthouse on a treacherous sea. People can't turn away from a message like that because they've never heard a message like that. All the world knows is for pain and complaining to go hand in hand. The more you hurt, the more complaining they expect to hear. But when you choose to lift up God's Word rather than your own, people take note.

Obviously, Sarah and I didn't do this perfectly, but in the moments when we did steward our platform well, doors were opened and hearts were softened. Doctors, nurses, family members, and friends all listened intently as we shared the hope we had in the face of the heartache we felt. Life was hard, but God was good.

Corrie ten Boom summed it up best, "In darkness God's truth shines most clear." The deeper the pain, the more pronounced His peace. Like a blazing star on a pitch-black night, every setback only serves to brighten the hope of Christ in us, every scar only serves to crank our megaphones louder, and every hurt only serves to elevate our platforms higher.

> "Always be prepared to give an answer to everyone who asks you to give the reason for the hope that you have."
> - 1 Peter 3:15

Discussion Questions:

1. What are some practical ways you can leverage your platform (e.g., social media, sharing with a friend, etc.)?
2. Who are the people who could benefit from hearing the story of God's faithfulness in your time of suffering?
3. What are three key truths you would remind someone who is going through a similar season of scarring as you?

Lesson #6:

He's not penalizing you, He's preparing you

"The strength of patience hangs on our capacity to believe that God is up to something good for us in all our delays and detours."
- John Piper

We live in a society where the severity of a punishment is supposed to fit the seriousness of the crime. That is to say, punishments should be fair. For example, if you drive a few miles over the speed limit, a slap on the wrist and a dent in your wallet would suffice. However, if you rob a bank, vandalize a police car, or race through a school zone, the size of your fine (and time spent in jail) would skyrocket. The greater the crime, the longer the punishment.

As we continued to wade past the one-month mark in the NICU I began to wonder if God operated by the same "the punishment matches the crime" system. *"Was God penalizing us for something we did wrong? Was Remi's disease a result of some sin we were walking in? Was He mad at us?"*

This seemed to be the only logical conclusion as every glimmer of hope was weekly dashed by Remi's test results. These disappointing genetic tests, blood work samples, and CT scans all continued to stretch our faith as well as our stay in the NICU. I began to question whether this pain was truly a platform to maximize or a punishment to endure. *"Is God penalizing me?"*

While I wish I could tell you the Lord answered these questions with an audible word, He didn't. Instead, as He often did during our six-week stint in the NICU, God answered with example after example from His written Word. It seemed that everywhere I flipped to in the Bible, the Spirit gently reminded my weary soul of this refreshing truth: the presence of pain doesn't necessarily mean there is a sin to *punish*, but a heart to *prepare*. Is suffering ever a result of sin? Absolutely. But just because God takes somebody the long way doesn't always mean He's done with them; it might just mean He's still developing them.

Exodus 13 embodies this principle perfectly. This chapter is sandwiched between two extremely well-known stories in the Israelites' exodus from Egypt: The Passover (Exodus 12) and the parting of the Red Sea (Exodus 14). However, while Exodus 13 may not be as well-known as its neighboring chapters, it's what God does in this stretch of verses that makes the rest of the Israelites' journey to the promised land possible. It reads,

> "When Pharaoh let the [Israelites] go, God did not lead them on the road through the Philistine country, **though that was shorter**. For God said, 'If they face war, **they might change their minds and return to Egypt.**' So God led the people around by the desert road toward the Red Sea. The Israelites went up out of Egypt ready for battle." (Exodus 13:17–18, emphasis mine)

The Lord purposefully extended the Israelites' exodus to corral their fear and build their faith. God knew if the Israelites took the fastest route to the promised land, they would have been confronted by the powerful Philistines and scurried back to the "comfort" of Egyptian slavery. Therefore, in His love for His people, God took the Israelites the long way.

But the Israelites didn't understand the necessity of this detour. Notice how the final verse in this passage describes their departure: "The Israelites went up out of Egypt **ready for battle**" (Exodus 13:18, emphasis mine). This confident bunch was armored up and fired up. They had just seen the most powerful nation in the world cry "Uncle!" without having to lift a finger. They were ready to take down anyone and everyone who dared to cross them...or so they thought.

Fast-forward just several verses later and the Israelites got a chance to see just how "ready for battle" they truly were:

> "The Lord hardened the heart of Pharaoh king of Egypt, so that he pursued the Israelites, who were marching out boldly. The Egyptians—all Pharaoh's horses and chariots, horsemen and troops—pursued the Israelites and overtook them as they camped by the sea near Pi Hahiroth, opposite Baal Zephon" (Exodus 14:8–9).

This should have been the moment the "bold" (Exodus 14:8) and "battle ready" (Exodus 13:18) Israelites were waiting for. After all, why wear all of that armor if you're not actually going to use it? Here was their chance to put some substance behind all of that swagger they supposedly had. It was time for the rubber to meet the road.

Of course, when push came to shove, the Israelites' confidence melted away like a popsicle on a hot summer day...just as the Lord predicted:

> "As Pharaoh approached, the Israelites looked up, and there were the Egyptians, marching after them. They were terrified and cried out to the Lord. They said to Moses, 'Was it because there were no graves in Egypt that you brought us to the desert to die? What have you done to us by bringing us out of Egypt? Didn't we say to you in Egypt, "Leave us alone; let us serve the Egyptians"? It would have been better for us to serve the Egyptians than to die in the desert!'" (Exodus 14:10–12).

While the Egyptians were still a long way off, the Israelites already admitted defeat. They had their white flags out and were waving them furiously. It turned out the Israelites weren't as "ready for battle" as they thought they were.

Herein lies God's heart behind taking the Israelites the long way. Had He allowed the Israelites to take the shortcut towards the promised land like they wanted, they would have been frightened by the Philistines and cowered before the Canaanites. They may have saved some time, but they would have forfeited the promised land.

Knowing this would have been the case, God, in His perfect love and wisdom, took His people the long way. He wasn't penalizing them, He was preparing them. Before they could arrive at the promised land, they needed to arrive at a spot of utter humility in their abilities and total confidence in God's. This lesson couldn't be skipped nor could it be learned in the fast lane. Only the long way could impart this truth. Sure, their dreams may have been delayed, but without the long way, their dreams would have been destroyed. The long way simply prepared them to receive what they had already been promised. Truly, their "detours" turned out to be His deliverance.

The pages of Scripture are filled with countless more examples of this "long way principle". A 40-year old Moses may have **thought** he was ready to deliver the Israelites from Egypt when he killed an abusive slave-master (see Exodus 2:11-12), but he wasn't. He needed the following 40 years of shepherding his father-in-law's sheep to learn how to shepherd his heavenly Father's people. The palace in Egypt couldn't teach him this lesson, only the long way could.

Similarly, a young teenage David must have felt ready to take the throne when he was anointed as the king-in-waiting way back in 1 Samuel 16, but he wasn't. He needed all of those years of running from King Saul to learn how to run a country.

LESSON SIX

He needed all those sleepless nights hiding from his enemies to learn how to hide in the Lord. The throne of Jerusalem couldn't teach him those lessons, only the long way could.

Finally, Satan must have assumed Jesus wanted the crown without going through the cross when he tempted Him in Matthew 4:8–10, but he was wrong. More than wanting to stockpile power, Jesus wanted to save His people. More than wanting relaxation for Himself, He wanted reconciliation for all mankind. The throne of heaven couldn't give Him these desires, only the long way up a hill called Calvary could.

The more you read the Bible, the more convinced you will become that God doesn't necessarily take His children the long way to *penalize* them, but to *prepare* them. He isn't holding out on us when a trial tarries, He's helping us. Shortcuts may be easier, but the long way is better.

While it was great to see this concept play out on the pages of Scripture, I wanted to see what this truth looked like in my own life. Where had I personally seen the benefit of delayed dreams and diverted desires in the past? Where had I seen the Lord take me the long way though I was "ready" for the next stage of life right there and then? Let me share just two of the many examples I recalled.

Towards the end of college, I was ready to be married...or so I thought. I had seen *The Notebook* and taken a walk or two on a sandy beach, what more could I need!? The only thing holding me back from getting married, my 22-year old mind reasoned, were a few "minor" issues I was dealing with. You know, "small" things like not pursuing the Lord on a daily basis, being extremely selfish with my time, and only being a mere three or four months removed from a nine-year addiction to pornography. Beyond those "minute" details, I was ready to go! All I needed was for the Lord to hold up on His end of the deal. Little did I know, however, God "holding up His end

67

of the deal" looked like providing me a long way to traverse rather than a lovely woman to marry.

Though this frustrated me at the time – *"Why is God holding out on me? What's taking Him so long to find a girl for me? Why is this such a long journey?"* – I can't express how grateful I am that the Lord took me the long way before meeting Sarah. I needed every single day of being single to grow and mature into a man who would be semi-worthy of dating and marrying a girl of Sarah's caliber. Had she met me as a 22-year old, she would rightfully have a different last name today. The Lord took me the long way to prepare me, not punish me.

An even better example comes from my desire to have kids. While Sarah and I were engaged, we both agreed having kids early on in marriage sounded like a great idea. Psalm 127:3 says, "Children are a heritage from the Lord, offspring a reward from him," so why not cash in on our reward as soon as possible? Therefore, two short months into marriage, voila, Sarah got pregnant. We were ready...or so we thought.

But after eight weeks of excitement and expectancy, Sarah had a miscarriage. The death of our first baby crushed our hearts but only heightened our dreams. Now more than ever we desperately wanted to have a baby. We felt as though we needed to make up for "lost time" we would have had with our previous child. But as pregnancy test after pregnancy test came back negative, it became extremely evident the Lord was taking us the long way.

This season was filled with heartbreak and heaviness. *"Why is the Lord holding out on us? Why is this taking so long? Will we ever get to become parents?"*

Knowing what we now know about Remi's dramatic entrance into this world, however, I couldn't be more thankful for the long way. For starters, Remi would not even exist had the Lord not taken us the long way through a miscarriage. The timeline between Sarah's first pregnancy and her second pregnancy with Remi would have overlapped, thus making the conception and creation of Remi an impossibility. I can't imagine what our lives would be like without our sweet little girl.

Secondly, had God allowed our first child to undergo the same pain and prognosis as Remi, our faith would have been a house of cards. One bad diagnosis, let alone the seemingly hundreds Remi had, would have been enough to cave our faith and consume us with fears. God used the long way through the miscarriage to strengthen our hearts and equip us for what was ahead. He wasn't penalizing us, He was preparing us.

What we needed when we first got married was not a baby, but a strong foundation. This strength couldn't be forged in the church pews or in the classroom, it had to be developed along the long way. These detours forced us to wrestle with the goodness of God in the face of our broken situation. It was in these valleys, and not the mountain peaks, where our character was solidified and our foundation was strengthened. This couldn't have been accomplished overnight, it required us to take the long way.

While this newfound understanding didn't solve Remi's health issues or allow us to go home any earlier, it sure did ease my fears. It reminded me that sometimes God has to fight *against* us in order to fight *for* us. Sometimes He needs to delay our dreams so He can prepare our hearts. He never holds out on us; He simply loves us too much to give us what we want without equipping us beforehand. He takes us the long way so our character can catch up with our ambitions and our foundation can support our dreams.

The long way may be wearisome today, but we must trust it will be worth it tomorrow.

"My son, do not despise the Lord's discipline, and do not resent his rebuke, because the Lord disciplines those he loves, as a father the son he delights in."
- Proverbs 3:11–12

Discussion Questions:

1. Where have you seen the blessing of the "long way" in your own life?
2. What "long way" might God have you on right now?
    a. How have you seen growth throughout this journey thus far?
    b. What practical steps can you take to remain faithful as you travel the long way?

Lesson #7:

Perseverance is an attitude to adopt, not an action to take

"Patience is more than endurance. A saint's life is in the hands of God like a bow and arrow in the hands of an archer. God is aiming at something the saint cannot see, and He stretches and strains, and every now and again the saint says—'I cannot stand anymore.' God does not heed, He goes on stretching till His purpose is in sight, then He lets fly. Trust yourself in God's hands. Maintain your relationship to Jesus Christ by the patience of faith. 'Though He slay me, yet will I trust in Him.'"
- Oswald Chambers

THE day had finally arrived. After six grueling weeks of uncertainty and anticipation, Remi finally had a promising CT scan. Though the disease was still present, Takayasu's arteritis was no longer spreading through the rest of her precious little body. The disease that threatened Remi's life, scarred her arteries, and largely shut down her right kidney was finally under control!

This highly anticipated news meant the long-awaited day was here at last. We were finally going home! For the first time in Remi's six-week life, we could remove all the cords from her body. For the first time since she was born, we could drive home as a family. And for the first time since we had become parents, we could sleep in the same room as our sweet baby. We couldn't have been more excited!

But then we got home and reality sank in. Though we were away from the dings and beeps of the NICU, many of its rhythms still followed us. We still manually took her blood pressure three times a day, administered medications at 7am, 1pm, and 7pm, called the doctors in St. Louis and Branson on a regular basis, and had Remi quarantined from the outside world for the majority of the next two months.

Additionally, now that we were away from the "safety net" of the hospital, every little cough, cry, and complaint Remi let out caused our minds to race with anxiety. We didn't want to be over-dramatic first-time parents, but we also didn't want to miss any sign Remi's health was taking a turn for the worse. After all, we couldn't Google, "*Why is our 6-week old baby with Takayasu's arteritis crying?*" because there were no other 6-week old babies with Takayasu's arteritis to compare with. We were in a new environment but still dealing with many of the same stresses and questions as before.

Please don't get me wrong, we LOVED being home! It was so nice to sleep in our own bed, have our own space, and have our own baby all to ourselves. There were no more doctors to examine her, needles to prick her, or noises to keep her up. We had longed for this day for six straight weeks. I suppose I just had unrealistic expectations of what home would truly be like. I naively thought when we left the hospital, we would be leaving our problems behind as well. Little did I know, when I strapped Remi into her car seat that day, I was also strapping in Takayasu's arteritis along with the truckload of worries, fears, and doubts that accompanied it. Many of the same problems we faced in the hospital would still be present at home. Our hearts would still hurt, our pain would still persist, and the "long way" would still drag on.

Herein lies the true difficulty of suffering. It's often not the *degree* of pain that gets us, it's the *duration*. Most of us can endure moments of excruciating pain (i.e., giving birth, undergoing surgery, or watching yet another *Hallmark Channel* Christmas movie with the exact same plot) with relative joy so long as we know there is an expiration date approaching. The difficulty of suffering, though, is the indefinite timetable we're often forced to live through.

This sets pain uniquely apart from almost anything else we experience in life. A marathon may be tough, but at least you get to stop running after 26.2 miles. Your job may be taxing, but at least there's the promise of a restful weekend ahead. And long road trips may drain you, but at least you know exactly how much time you have remaining in the car.

The pathway of pain, however, offers no rest for the weary. There's no obvious or tangible finish line to work towards. Your "race" through heartache doesn't end after 26.2 miles; you must keep running. You don't get to take a few days off after a long week of suffering; pain stays with you. And you don't get to look at your GPS and know when your trial will terminate; you just have to keep putting one foot in front of the other. Like the pounding surf or a persistent shadow, pain seemingly never tires nor goes away.

This relentless nature of pain makes stamina, not speed, the primary quality to possess. Like the tortoise from *The Tortoise and the Hare* or the train from *The Little Engine That Could*, life doesn't favor those with the most giftings, it favors those with the most grit.

"Grit" is the ability to press forward despite difficult circumstances. It's the ability to keep on getting up after you've been knocked down. The Bible labels this indispensable quality as "perseverance" and pulls no punches when donning it as the chief attribute to possess when enduring pain. Let me show you just three examples:

> "...we also glory in our sufferings, because we know that suffering produces **perseverance; perseverance**, character; and character, hope. And hope does not put us to shame, because

God's love has been poured out into our hearts through the Holy Spirit." Romans 5:3–5 (emphasis mine)

"Consider it pure joy, my brothers and sisters, whenever you face trials of many kinds, because you know that the testing of your faith produces **perseverance**. Let **perseverance** finish its work so that you may be mature and complete, not lacking anything." James 1:2–4 (emphasis mine)

"Blessed is the one who **perseveres** under trial because, having stood the test, that person will receive the crown of life that the Lord has promised to those who love him."
James 1:12 (emphasis mine)

Perseverance is clearly a trait highly regarded by the Lord, but let me ask you a question: What does this crucial characteristic look like, practically speaking, in the heat of a trial? In other words, what tangible steps must you take in order to persevere?

This question is easy to answer when looking at a marathon – to persevere is to complete the race. However, if you chose not to persevere through the marathon, the race would stop; you wouldn't have to keep going. Similarly, if you persevered through a weight-lifting exercise, you would complete the rep. Failing to persevere would result in the bar being lifted from your weary body; you wouldn't have to keep lifting.

But what does it look like to persevere through an *actual trial*? You know, marital strife, unemployment, or a sick child where there's no real finish line to work towards or timetable to compete against? Does one need an unbroken prayer life to embody the type of perseverance described in Romans 5:3–5? If so, for how long? Does one need a stellar church attendance to obtain the prize of perseverance in James 1:2–4? If so, how many Sundays are you "allowed" to miss and still maintain this excellent standing? Or perhaps one must embark on a 40-day fast to possess a James 1:12-perseverance. Surely *this* is how perseverance is practically lived out in the life of a believer, right?

As I struggled to find an answer for these questions, the obscurity of perseverance became a great source of anxiety when I considered my own grit (or lack thereof) in Remi's situation. Was I actually persevering like the Lord wanted me to? What did it *practically* look like for me to *metaphorically* put one foot in front of the other? What finish line was I moving towards? If I continued to read my Bible, tithe my money, take Remi's blood pressure, give Remi her meds, and take her to St. Louis for her monthly doctor appointments, was I displaying perseverance or was I still missing the mark?

To make this inquiry more complicated, a failure to persevere on my end wouldn't have obvious, tangible manifestations. It's not like doctors would burst into Remi's room the moment I stopped persevering and say, "Wow, it looks like Remi's disease is miraculously gone. She's totally healed now!" The burden may be removed in a race or exercise when we fail to persevere, but pain plays by different rules. Takayasu's arteritis was still going to threaten my sweet Remi's life regardless of my grit or lack thereof.

I imagine the same ambiguity accompanies your own scars as well. What, after all, does perseverance practically look like for you? Or perhaps a better question to consider is what difference does perseverance actually make? Will the bank cancel your debts the moment you stop persevering in monthly payments? No way! Will your marriage suddenly improve the moment you stop persevering in kindness? Not a chance! Will your prodigal child return home the moment you stop persevering in prayer? Certainly not! What difference, then, does perseverance actually make? And more significantly, how does one practically live out biblical perseverance?

In answering this two-part question, we need only to look back at our verses above. While perseverance may not guarantee tangible rewards such as a higher credit score or lower cholesterol, it nevertheless brings about an undeniable change in our lives. Namely, we're told that the person who perseveres will become, "...mature and complete" (James 1:1–4), will obtain the, "...crown of life" (James 1:12), and will possess a, "...hope [that] does not put us to shame" (Romans 5:3–5).

Can you physically hold any of these benefits in your hand? No. But do these intangibles make a tangible difference? You better believe it! One who is "mature and complete" is able to love his or her spouse immeasurably more than an immature version of themselves. One who knows that the "crown of life" awaits them is free to run after Jesus, not money, a promotion, or the cares of this world. And one who has a "hope that does not put us to shame" cannot be shaken by the ups and downs of life.

The way the authors of Scripture see it, we all have to go through trials whether we like it or not, so why not obtain these rewards along the way? If you're forced to have cancer, why not grow in character? If you're losing money, why not acquire maturity? And if your health is fading like a shadow, why not have a hope that shines like the sun? Pain will still take you through the "Valley of the Shadow of Death," but perseverance will hand you a "gift bag" on the other side.

Of course, if one wants to receive the *rewards* of perseverance, one must first do the *requirements* of perseverance. This, again, is where we run into trouble. The benefits of perseverance are printed in black and white but the "Thou must do this" or "Thou mustn't do that" to persevere are nowhere to be found in these verses. Why so much vagueness? Why don't these verses just come right out and tell us plainly what we need to do?

Perhaps these verses appear to be obscure only because we're asking them to offer us something God never promised in the first place. While we want to know what *action* to take, the Bible is interested in something far different. Take one more look with me at these verses to see what I mean:

> "...we also **glory in our sufferings**, because we know that suffering produces perseverance."
> Romans 5:3–5 (emphasis mine)

> "Consider it **pure joy**...whenever you face trials of many kinds, because you know that the testing of your faith produces perseverance."
> James 1:2–3 (emphasis mine)

> "**Blessed** [or "happy"] is the one who perseveres under trial."
> James 1:12 (emphasis mine)

Three times in three separate verses we're not told what *actions* to take but what *attitude* to adopt. In other words, to persevere through a trial is to have joy through a trial.

This turns our concept of perseverance on its head. We are accustomed to *doing* this or *doing* that to display perseverance. For example, a marathon runner displays perseverance by crossing the finish line. Regardless of how good, bad, or ugly their attitude was throughout the 26.2-mile race, if they cross the finish line, particularly if they cross the finish line *first*, people will say they showed a tremendous amount of perseverance.

However, the same does not hold true for a Christian. I can take Remi's blood pressure, administer medications, take her to St. Louis, change her diapers, wash her clothes, and call her doctors, but unless it is done with a joyful attitude, I'm not pleasing God, I'm actually offending Him. My non-joyful (i.e., "complaining") attitude is nothing more than a tangible manifestation of my lack of trust in His infinite wisdom. It is simply a wicked and demonic declaration that I would be a better god than He is.

Therefore, perseverance *for* God is only possible where there is first trust *in* God. Unless we grasp Lessons #1–6, we can't truly display biblical perseverance. No amount of "right" actions can override this reality. Don't get me wrong, though, our actions are still very important. Perseverance still demands we continue to pray, go to counseling, take medications, and the like. But in order for all of these actions to be God-honoring and grit-exuding, they must first be draped in the right attitude.

As a result, biblical perseverance is a battle that begins in our minds. It looks like taking another step towards our God before we take another step towards our goal. It means we must first fight for contentment before fighting for completion. What it ultimately means, then, is far more than beating cancer, beating the budget, or beating the odds, perseverance is beating our fears because we trust in our God. It's not a destination to arrive at or a goal to check off our list, it's an attitude to embrace and a mindset to adopt.

This elusive concept becomes easier to grasp if we zoom out beyond the concept of perseverance for just a moment. Time and time again throughout the Scriptures you'll find the Lord emphasizing the state of mankind's hearts over and beyond the work of their hands. Case in point is 1 Samuel 16:7, "The Lord does not look at the things people look at. People look at the outward appearance, but the Lord looks at the heart." God not only looks at *what* we do, He looks at *how* or *why* we do it.

This idea carried over into the New Testament and became the overarching theme of Christ's first major sermon in the book of Matthew (Matthew 5–7). Whether it was regarding our relationships with others (Matthew 5:21–26, 43–48), our sexual purity (Matthew 5:27–30), our acts of generosity (Matthew 6:1–4) or even our prayer life (Matthew 6:5–15), Christ consistently stressed His interest in the attitudes of our hearts over the surface level works of our hands.

Luke 21:1–4 shows just one instance of this principle in action. As Jesus watched people tithe their money in the temple, He noticed a poor widow giving two small copper coins while a group of wealthy individuals were pouring in mountains of cash. Though it would make sense for the Son of God to favor those who gave the most money to the temple of God, Jesus pulled a "1 Samuel 16:7" and showed preference to the humble attitude of the widow rather than the wads of cash from the wealthy. Apparently, Jesus was never interested in people's money, He was interested in their motives. Much like perseverance, Christ wanted to know *why* people were giving, not just *what* they were giving. The attitude of their hearts trumped the actions of their hands.

This "Attitude > Actions" realization brought so much freedom into my life as this season of scarring dragged on. Perseverance was no longer something I had to arrive at, it was something I got to rest in. It was not determined by the outcome of Remi's condition or the amount of actions I could accomplish but rather by the outlook of my heart. God wasn't grading me for how many prayers I could say nor was He asking me to shoulder this burden alone. He was inviting me in all my brokenness to lay my burdens at His feet – "Come to me, all you who are weary and burdened, and I will give you rest. Take my yoke upon you and learn from me, for I am gentle and humble in heart, and you will find rest for your souls" (Matthew 11:28–29). So long as I could maintain hope in Him, even as weak and pathetic as my faith often was, perseverance was possible because, as J.I. Packer once said, "Your faith will not fail while God sustains it; you are not strong enough to fall away while God is resolved to hold you."[1]

Christ's incredible burden-bearing invitation is extended to you as well. God isn't looking at all the religious tasks you've checked off your to-do list, He's looking first and foremost at your heart. Second Chronicles 16:9 puts it this way, "For the eyes of the Lord range throughout the earth to strengthen those whose hearts are fully committed to him...." Did you notice what brought about God's strength in this verse? It wasn't effort but belief – "to strengthen those **whose hearts are fully committed to him....**" In other words, the strength and perseverance *of* God are given to those who first have hope and trust *in* God. Again, perseverance is something we rest in, not reach for.

These time-tested, Scripture-saturated truths have been such an encouragement to Sarah and me as we wade through uncharted waters. Though our faith is still often so small, we are incredibly grateful that God's strength isn't limited by our weakness. It is actually magnified in it (2 Corinthians 12:9–10). He is the, "God [of] endurance" (Romans 15:5) who never grows, "...tired or weary" (Isaiah 40:28). Our shoes may wear out along the journey, but our God never will!

> "Do you not know? Have you not heard? The Lord is the everlasting God, the Creator of the ends of the earth. He will not grow tired or weary, and his understanding no one can fathom. He gives strength to the weary and increases the power of the weak.
> Even youths grow tired and weary, and young men stumble and fall; but those who hope in the Lord will renew their strength. They will soar on wings like eagles; they will run and not grow weary, they will walk and not be faint."
> Isaiah 40:28–31

---

[1] J.I. Packer Knowing God

Discussion Questions:

1. On a scale of 1–10 ("1" being awful and "10" being amazing), how positive and hopeful has your attitude been in times of recent trial?
2. What are some hurdles keeping you from persevering like you would like to?
3. What are some steps you can take to grow in perseverance?

Lesson #8:

Pain is the ugly wrapping paper on a beautiful gift

"Let me learn by paradox that the way down is the way up,
that to be low is to be high,
that the broken heart is the healed heart,
that the contrite spirit is the rejoicing spirit,
that the repenting soul is the victorious soul,
that to have nothing is to possess all,
that to bear the cross is to wear the crown,
that to give is to receive,
that the valley is the place of vision."
- A Puritan prayer from *The Valley of Vision*

Though our days in the NICU have become a faint dot in the rearview mirror, their memory still looms large in my mind. One cry from Remi and I'm right back in St. Louis waiting with bated breath before our first conference room meeting. One glance at an empty car seat and my mind recalls all the excruciating times I would look in the rearview mirror as we left the hospital only to see that same empty car seat staring back at me. And one high blood pressure reading and a pit begins to develop in my stomach as I reminisce on all the times Sarah and I played "doctor" on our screaming baby once safely back at home.

This has certainly been one thrilling season with some insane highs and gut-wrenching lows, but even as hard, trying, exhausting, nerve-racking, ulcer-inducing, and heartbreaking as this trial has been, the best descriptor I can think of to describe this season is a "gift."

A gift? Yes, you read that right—a gift. Granted, this season has been one of "those" gifts, but a gift, nevertheless. You know what "those" gifts are, don't you? Maybe it's a gym membership, a new vacuum cleaner, or a budgeting book from Dave Ramsey. "Those" gifts are the presents you know are good for you, but you just really don't care to receive. Five years down the road you may be grateful, but all you can think about in the moment is the fact that you received a *SlimFast* bar rather than a candy bar for Christmas. What a bummer!

That's a pretty good snapshot of what life has been like for us over the past few months. It's been hard, but it's been good. God has given incredible gifts such as an increased faith, a deeper appreciation of His power, and a stronger marriage but none of these gifts manifested themselves in the ways we thought they would. I assumed the opportunity to grow in my faith would be wrapped in the paper of a systematic theology textbook, not a bad test result for my daughter. I assumed a deeper appreciation of God's power would be wrapped in the paper of a Hillsong worship album, not an extended stay at the hospital. And I assumed the opportunity to strengthen my relationship with Sarah would be wrapped in the paper of a romantic vacation, not mutual heartbreak and desperate prayers each night.

But this is how the Lord often operates. He tends to wrap the most beautiful gifts in the ugliest of papers, pain being His chief paper of choice. The gift of trust is typically wrapped in the paper of a trial, the gift of intimacy is often wrapped in the paper of heartbreak, and the gift of salvation is always wrapped in the paper of the cross.

This ugly wrapping paper is why we so often walk right past what the Lord wants to give us. We all want favor and blessings, but very few are willing to dig through the pain-riddled wrapping paper to obtain these. We see a negative doctor's report, loss of a job, or strained relationship as something to complain to God about, not thank Him for. We take one look at His gift for us and storm away in fury because it's wrapped in the paper of singleness, infertility, or loneliness. "God's holding out on me!" we exclaim, while never taking the time to unwrap what's inside.

I know this to be the case because this was sadly my m.o. throughout our time in the NICU. My "Amazon Wish List" on the morning of March 18th included items such as a growing intimacy with the Lord, a deeper relationship with Sarah, and a greater appreciation for Remi, not Takayasu's arteritis or six weeks in the hospital. Therefore, upon receiving these gifts, I angrily scrambled for a return receipt — "This isn't what I wanted, God! Fix this!"

What I didn't understand at the time, however, was the latter was being used to bring about the former. God was using my pain to not only give me what I asked for, but to give me *immeasurably* more than I asked for (Ephesians 3:20). I wanted safety, He wanted dependence. I wanted normalcy, He wanted nearness. I wanted a healthy baby, He wanted a healthy fear of the Lord. I wanted comfort, He wanted closeness. Ultimately, the Lord didn't just use my pain to bring about *some* presents (i.e., "gifts"), He used it to bring about *His* presence (i.e., "nearness").

I'm not sure if any biblical character grasped this concept quite like Paul. By his own count in 2 Corinthians 11:24–27 (ESV), Paul had been flogged five times, beaten with rods three times, stoned one time, shipwrecked three times, and was constantly, "...in danger from rivers, danger from robbers, danger from my own people, danger from Gentiles, danger in the city, danger in the wilderness, danger at sea, danger from false brothers; in toil and hardship, through many a sleepless night, in hunger and thirst, often without food, in cold and exposure."

If that's not bad enough, Paul continued to roll up his sleeves to reveal more scars in 2 Corinthians 12:7, "...I was given a thorn in my flesh, a messenger of Satan, to torment me." If Paul were alive today, I'm not sure many people would want to be friends with a guy as "snake bitten" (both metaphorically and literally – see Acts 28:1–6) as he was.

Understandably so, Paul pleaded with the Lord multiple times in 2 Corinthians 12:8 to remove these thorn-laced trials from his life. But rather than changing Paul's circumstances, the Lord changed Paul's outlook. This very same apostle who formerly wanted nothing to do with pain concluded this long list of woes by saying he now, "delight[ed] in weaknesses, in insults, in hardships, in persecutions, in difficulties" (2 Corinthians 12:10). Rather than running from pain, it's almost as if Paul channeled his inner Br'er Rabbit and ran to the thorn-heavy "briar patch." He was not just content with his thorns, he actually "boasted" in them (2 Corinthians 12:9). Why was this the case? What had happened between 2 Corinthians 12:7 and 12:9 that caused such a dramatic paradigm shift within Paul?

The larger context of this passage gives us our answer:

> "...I [Paul] was given a thorn in my flesh, a messenger of Satan, to torment me. Three times I pleaded with the Lord to take this away from me. But He said to me, 'My grace is sufficient for you, for my power is made perfect in weakness.' Therefore I will boast all the more gladly in my weaknesses, so that Christ's power may rest on me. That is why, for Christ's sake, I delight in weaknesses, in insults, in hardships, in persecutions, in difficulties. For when I am weak, then I am strong." (2 Corinthians 12:7–10)

Paul's transformed attitude sprung from his transcendent understanding that pain was nothing more than the ugly wrapping paper on the beautiful gifts of God. His brokenness, bruises, and bumps all certainly hurt, but Paul soon discovered these pains were merely the avenues through which his debilitating weaknesses could be exchanged for God's infinite strength — "For when I am weak, then I am strong." Furthermore, it was the very presence of these nagging ailments in the first place that regularly drove the apostle to his knees, which in turn regularly drove him into the presence of the Almighty — "Three times I pleaded with the Lord...." The more pain he had, the closer proximity to God he experienced.

Had the Lord numbed Paul's heartache like he asked for in 2 Corinthians 12:7, the apostle would have forfeited the source of his relational and ministerial might. His life might have been more peaceful, but it would have been less powerful. He would have had more of his health, but less of the Holy One. No wonder Paul "boast[ed] all the more gladly in [his] weaknesses"! They weren't problems to complain about but invitations to embrace.

We adopt a similar mindset when we see our scars and sufferings through the same lens as Paul did. The apostle knew his pain in and of itself was not a gift (i.e., persecution wasn't a gift, nor was his poverty), but what it brought about certainly was (i.e., the power and presence of God). Therefore, Paul viewed his pain as nothing more than a FedEx delivery truck by which the Lord delivered His greatest gifts to Paul's life. It was merely the avenue through which the apostle got to experience the power and presence of God unlike never before.

This is crucial for us to understand. Our scars (i.e., cancer, death, loneliness, etc.) aren't intrinsically gifts in and of themselves, but they do bring about gifts. These gifts may not be wrapped in the paper of comfort or ease, but our richest moments with God are rarely forged in the seasons of abundance. When life gives us a La-Z-Boy, we tend to rest in the La-Z-Boy; when life gives us a thorn, we have no choice but to rest in the Almighty. Pain, therefore, should not be viewed as a hurdle to happiness but rather as a key to the heart of God. It moves the Lord from being something to be *explained* to Someone to be *experienced*.

You could say pain is to our relationship with God what a taste test is to our understanding of food. Before you sink your teeth into a dish you may know what other people have said about the food, but that's merely secondhand information. In order to truly understand what something tastes like, you must try it for yourself.

In the same way, times of abundance tend to restrict our relationship with God to a secondhand concept to be understood rather than a loving Father to be worshipped. We may read about God's power for the weak (2 Corinthians 12:9–10), His nearness to the brokenhearted (Psalm 34:18), and His all-encompassing peace in times of trial (Philippians 4:6–7), but comfort and success hardly ever allow these truths to transfer from our head to our heart. Instead, all we're left with is information *about* God rather than intimacy *with* God.

Pain, on the other hand, is a spiritual "taste test" that enables us to truly, "Taste and see that the Lord is good" (Psalm 34:8). We no longer have to take a pastor's or parent's word for it, we see these spiritual truths transform into tangible realities before our very eyes. This is why Job concluded his lengthy season of suffering by saying to the Lord, "My ears have heard of you but now my eyes have seen you" (Job 42:5). Job's secondhand knowledge of God became a firsthand experience of His power and presence.

The primary way pain accomplishes this task is by magnifying our need for God. While utter helplessness isn't a goal many of us naturally run after, it just so happens to be exactly what God is looking for. In Isaiah 57:15 the Lord declares, "...I live in a high and holy place, but also with the one who is contrite and lowly in spirit." Did you catch that? The Lord's presence primarily presides in two places: a "high and holy place" and with those who possess a "contrite and lowly...spirit." In other words, if you want to be close to God, you need to put as much distance between yourself and pride. The access code to the heart of God is "H-U-M-I-L-I-T-Y."

I don't know if you've noticed or not but it's nearly impossible to maintain a truly humble and dependent state when you have everything you need. A comfortable and complacent heart tends to follow the same destructive pattern as King Uzziah in 2 Chronicles 26:16 (ESV), "But when he was strong, he grew proud, to his destruction." Getting a bonus, getting married, or getting upgraded to first class tends to make us more reliant on ourselves, not on the Lord. After all, why would we need a Savior if we don't need to be saved from anything?

When pain is present, however, this mindset shifts. Our wounds highlight our weaknesses and our heartache amplifies our helplessness. We can no longer exist under the mirage that we are strong enough or wise enough to conquer our problems on our own. Our scars help us recognize our deep sense of frailty and desperate need for something or Someone else to help us. Perhaps an illustration of this process might be beneficial.

If you were lifting weights and had a spotter behind you, when would the spotter begin to help? Well, if they were a good spotter, they wouldn't lend assistance until you were at a point where you could no longer lift the bar by your own strength. So long as you keep pushing and making progress, the spotter's strength would not enter the equation. However, when your arms could no longer bear the weight on your own, then and only then would a good spotter step in and use their strength to remove the burden from you.

In the same way, God largely withholds His power so long as we try to stress and strain through life by our own strength. Psalm 127:1 (emphasis mine) colorfully describes our feeble self-sufficient efforts by saying, "Unless the Lord builds the house, the builders labor in vain. Unless the Lord watches over the city, the guards stand watch in vain." Our best efforts are vanity at best and sinful at worst. However, when we reach the end of our strength, God's unbridled power – much like that of a spotter – comes flooding into our lives.

The sad reality, then, is when we as Christians try to avoid any and everything that will push us beyond the threshold of our strength, little knowing this act of self-preservation costs us the very power of God. However, not willing that we should miserably continue with this sinful and slothful attitude, God, in His sovereign wisdom and unsearchable love, allows pain into our lives so we might be forced out of our comfort zone and into the power of His Spirit. It is our blessed pain, then, that activates the strength of our Spotter and drives us to pray, our weakness that leads us to worship, and our humility that ultimately brings us to the heart of the Healer.

The author of Proverbs 30:8–9 understood this fully when he prayed, "Keep falsehood and lies far from me; give me neither poverty nor riches, but give me only my daily bread. Otherwise, I may have too much and disown you and say, 'Who is the Lord?' Or I may become poor and steal, and so dishonor the name of my God." This man asked for, no, *begged for*, just two things before he died: *truthfulness* and *dependence*. "Don't give me too much otherwise I'll disown You," he said. "And don't give me too little or I'll dishonor You. Just give me enough to keep my head above water. Let me live paycheck to paycheck so I'll remain totally dependent upon You."

Who prays like this? Who actually *wants* to feel their desperate need for God? Don't we tend to say everything in our prayers and do everything in our power to feel the exact opposite? But this man prayed for dependence rather than abundance because he understood, as A.W. Tozer so eloquently put it, "The importance of coming into God's presence is worth overcoming all obstacles along the way."[1] If Psalm 16:11 (ESV) is true – "...in your presence there is fullness of joy; at your right hand are pleasures forevermore" – then any obstacle to this gift is merely the price of admission and a price well worth paying. Hurt leads to humility, which ultimately leads us to the Healer.

This sequence of events is one that I've seen consistently play out since Remi was born. Whether it's wrapped in the paper of high blood pressure or long days at the hospital, the Lord has used Takayasu's arteritis to regularly bring me to the end of myself that I might find the foot of the cross. He's used this season to remind me the best way to bow *up* to my problems is by first bowing *down* to His ability. He's reminded me that the "easiest way" often isn't the "best way." And while I haven't become a glutton for pain who celebrates sleepless nights with a screaming baby or long medical bills, He's reminded me that what is brought about because of the "briar patch" is of far greater worth than any fleeting pleasure the world could offer me.

Joni Eareckson Tada can relate. Having been born into an athletic family, Joni enjoyed running, swimming, and doing everything under the sun until a diving accident as a 17-year old paralyzed Joni from the shoulders down. Joni was understandably devastated when she learned she would spend the rest of her life confined to a wheelchair and admittedly struggled with serious depression for several years. However, the Lord eventually softened Joni's heart and gave her the ability to see the gift pain was ushering into her life. Her own words best describe her new perspective in her booklet *Hope...the Best of Thing*:[2]

---

[1] A.W. Tozer Experiencing the Presence of God: Teachings from the Book of Hebrews

> "I sure hope I can bring this wheelchair to heaven.
>
> Now, I know that's not theologically correct.
>
> But I hope to bring it and put it in a little corner of heaven, and then in my new, perfect, glorified body, standing on grateful glorified legs, I'll stand next to my Savior, holding his nail-pierced hands.
>
> I'll say, 'Thank you, Jesus,' and he will know that I mean it, because he knows me.
>
> He'll recognize me from the fellowship we're now sharing in his sufferings.
>
> And I will say, 'Jesus, do you see that wheelchair? You were right when you said that in this world we would have trouble, because that thing was a lot of trouble. But the weaker I was in that thing, the harder I leaned on you. And the harder I leaned on you, the stronger I discovered you to be. It never would have happened had you not given me the bruising of the blessing of that wheelchair.'"

Much like the apostle Paul, Joni counted her most severe scars as her biggest blessings. The disabilities that handicapped her health were used by God to empower her spirit and provide her with a platform. In fact, Joni's ministry – "Joni and Friends" (www.joniandfriends.org) – in which Joni ministers to millions of disabled children and adults every year wouldn't even exist if it were not for that fateful day as a 17-year old. No wonder she's able to say "Thank you, Jesus" when reflecting on all the gifts the Lord has brought about through this hardship.

---

[2] Taken from Hope...the Best of Things by Joni Eareckson Tada, © 2008, pp. 29. Used by permission of Crossway, a publishing ministry of Good News Publishers, Wheaton, IL 60187, www.crossway.org.

I love how Joni concludes this section:

> "So thank you for what you did in my life through that wheelchair. And now...you can send that wheelchair to hell, if you want."[3]

What an incredible (and hilarious) exclamation to wrap up her thoughts! If intimacy with Jesus is truly the greatest gift we could ask for, then pain is not something to complain about, it's something to "glory" (Romans 5:3) and "boast" in (2 Corinthians 12:9); it's something to "consider...pure joy" (James 1:2). Or to say it differently, if dependence is the goal, then weakness is an advantage.

Sarah and I continue to strive to see our pain through this lens. Takayasu's arteritis may have narrowed Remi's arteries, but it's expanded our faith. What other situation would have given us this blessing? What other situation would have allowed us to witness God defying medicine, death, and our own doubts time and time again? What other situation would have given us such confidence in our God? "The Lord is my light and my salvation—whom shall I fear? The Lord is the stronghold of my life—of whom shall I be afraid?" (Psalm 27:1).

Additionally, time in the NICU might as well have been the greatest "marriage conference" we could ever attend. We got to spend every single moment of every single day for six straight weeks together as we sat in the hospital with our sweet little Remi. What other situation would have enabled me to spend so much time with the woman I love? What other situation would have brought about so much growth? Thanks to our scars, our love is deeper, our unity is stronger, and our marriage is richer than ever before. "Though he slay me, yet will I hope in him" (Job 13:15).

---

[3] http://t.joniandfriends.org/radio/4-minute/holiest-wheelchairs/

Paul sums up my thoughts perfectly in Philippians 1:29 (emphasis mine), "For it has been **granted** to you on behalf of Christ not only to believe in him, but also to suffer for him." It has been "granted" to us to suffer, or as the New Living Translation puts it, we have been given, "...the **privilege** of suffering for him" (Philippians 1:29, NLT, emphasis mine). If Jesus truly is our prize and humility truly is the key, then pain becomes a privileged opportunity to embrace, not a pesky inconvenience to avoid.

I wonder what you would discover if you too were to look past the paper of conflict, cancer, or Crohn's to find the presents the Lord has provided underneath? What power has entered your life? What joy have you experienced? What proximity have you enjoyed? While pain is never fun, it also never leaves us empty handed. It is simply the funnel through which God's grace and nearness flow most freely. The deeper the hurt, the wider the funnel.

What a precious gift indeed!

"It was good for me to be afflicted so that I might learn your decrees."
- Psalm 119:71

Discussion questions:

1. Look back at a previous time of suffering. Can you identify any gifts that came about due to this trial?
2. How would remembering that every pain brings about the power and proximity of God change your attitude towards suffering?
3. Who is the godliest person you know? What trials have shaped them into the man or woman they are today?

To be continued...

"Faith never knows where it is being led, but it loves and knows the One who is leading."
- Oswald Chambers

A lot of people say they're really bad at goodbyes. Maybe you know someone like this or perhaps you are that type of person. Saying goodbye to a friend, to a season of life, or even to a piece of clothing you hardly ever wore is like nails across a chalkboard. Goodbyes kill you!

I, on the other hand, I'm actually pretty good at goodbyes. I'm not trying to toot my own horn or sound cocky, I just have never really had an issue moving on from anything. (Okay, there was that one time I cried after my childhood dog, Maverick, died when I moved off to college but come on, who *wouldn't* cry in that situation!?) I've just always been a non-sentimental, out-of-sight-out-of-mind-kinda guy who can "cut the cord" pretty easily and move on. (Alright, there was also that time when I learned that Tony Romo retired and my eyes started watering, but that was allergies...I promise!)

Strangely, though, it's been rather difficult for me to write the final chapter of this book. I was hoping to end this journey with a resounding exclamation point – "Remi is totally healed! Her disease is gone!" But instead of certainty, all I have to offer is more question marks. Remi still has Takayasu's arteritis (though doctors believe she is in a stable state), we still take her blood pressure daily, we still give her medicine in the morning and evening, we still take frequent trips to St. Louis

Children's Hospital, and we still don't know how her story will end.

This uncertainty makes ending the book right here feel a little like making cookie dough but never putting it in the oven – it's still good, it's just not done yet. There are still so many more questions to be answered and bridges to be crossed.

Here's what we do know, however. While uncertainty hangs like a heavy fog over Remi's future, we know Who's holding the pen and writing her story. We believe the author of Remi's life is the *Author of Life* (Acts 3:15). He isn't the frightful Edgar Allan Poe or the too-good-to-be-true Dr. Seuss. He is the, "... compassionate and gracious God, slow to anger, abounding in love and faithfulness, maintaining love to thousands, and forgiving wickedness, rebellion and sin. Yet he does not leave the guilty unpunished" (Exodus 34:6–7).

It's amazing what happens to our outlook when we remember how incredible an Author God truly is; it's a bit like riding a thrilling roller coaster. We may get tossed here, there, and everywhere, but we're able to enjoy the ride because we trust that somehow, someway, the designer of the ride has a purpose for every twist and every turn. In a similar sense, our fears are burned away like the morning mist when we remember the Designer of Remi's life is sovereignly in control of all the ups and downs and will ultimately work everything out for our good and His glory (Romans 8:28). A blank page with a good Author is a great recipe for an incredible story!

Who knows? Perhaps one day I'll be able to write a follow-up book that will have a lot more "!" than "?" in the conclusion. I long for that day to come!

Until then, Sarah and I are enjoying the ride with all the new friends we've made along the way. We still have a hard time wrapping our minds around how such a big God could use such a small girl to influence such a wide audience. I can't begin to tell you how many "strangers" I've met who have been earnestly praying for and greatly impacted by Remi's life. She is unquestionably the most popular and influential member of my family! (In case you were wondering, Sarah is a close second. I'm barely on the map but that's only because my mom is still in my corner. The rest of my family and friends quickly shifted to "Team Remi" from Day 1! Who can blame them!?)

I'm sincerely grateful for the prayers so many of you have showered my family with. Our journey through the NICU is like that of the Israelites in Exodus 17:8–13. As Joshua and the Israelites were fighting the Amalekites in the valley below, Moses was interceding on their behalf on the mountain above. "As long as Moses held up his hands, the Israelites were winning, but whenever he lowered his hands, the Amalekites were winning" (Exodus 17:11). Any of the "victories" we've experienced or strength we've displayed is fully accredited to the grace of the Lord and the countless number of men and women who faithfully held their hands high while we were waging war in our own valley.

As we end our journey together, I ask for you to continue to lift our family up in prayer. God has given us a platform and we don't want to waste it. We so desperately want those who hear our story to focus on the *Healer* of Remi, not the *healing* of Remi. His story is the only one worthy of our worship and admiration. May her story bring Jesus much glory!

Additionally, please continue bombarding God's throne for our sweet girl. We obviously want our little angel to be totally healed with no side effects or knowledge that anything was ever wrong with her. However, even more than physical health, we ask for you to pray for Remi's spiritual health. As Jesus once asked, "For what will it profit a man if he gains the whole world and forfeits his soul?" (Matthew 16:26, ESV). What good would it be for Remi to have a healthy body for 70–80 years but spend an eternity apart from the Lord? Please pray that Remi would be a woman of faith who genuinely loves the Lord and His people.

Finally, I want to leave you with the same burden I felt as I began to write this book. Second Corinthians 1:3–4 (emphasis mine) says, "Praise be to the God and Father of our Lord Jesus Christ, the Father of compassion and the God of all comfort, who comforts us in all our troubles, so that we can comfort those in any trouble with the comfort we ourselves receive from God." We are given comfort SO THAT we might pass it along, not keep it for ourselves.

If this book has been of any comfort to you, would you prayerfully consider passing it along to someone else? Or better yet, if the Lord comforted you in your own trial, would you consider writing a book or blog of your own? The avenue of your "so that" is not important, but obedience is. God desires for the lessons you've learned in the fire to be an encouragement to others as they traverse their own valleys. It doesn't need to be long or well written (let this book be your "Exhibit A" to that truth!), it simply needs to point others to Jesus. Again, His story is the only one worthy of our worship and admiration.

He's not just enough, He's more than enough!

> "Being confident of this, that he who began a good work in you
> will carry it on to completion until the day of Christ Jesus."
> - Philippians 1:6

TO BE CONTINUED...

Discussion Questions:

1. Which lesson (or chapter) from this book have you seen play out in your life? Which is the most difficult to apply?
2. What lesson(s) has the Lord personally taught you through your own trials?
3. How can you share the lessons you've learned with other people? Who might benefit from hearing your story?

If you have any thoughts or comments after reading this book, or if perhaps you've seen the Savior in your own scars, I would love to hear about it! Email me at seeingthesavior@gmail.com

Made in the USA
San Bernardino, CA
21 May 2020